DREAMHEALER

His name is

Adam.

He looks like a regular kid.
But at the age of 16, he is credited with
healing hundreds of people.
This is his own astonishing, true story...

Canadian Cataloging in Publication Data
ISBN: ISBN 0-9732748-0-8
Adam, 2003, DreamHealer
First Printing - April 2003
Printed and bound in Canada.
Second Printing - November 2003
Printed and bound in the United States.
All rights reserved.

Additional copies can be purchased at:
www.dreamhealer.com

Distributed by:
Hampton Roads Publishing Company
1125 Stoney Ridge Road
Charlottesville, VA 22902
800-766-8009
www.hrpub.com

The information contained in this book is not intended to be medical information. See your physician if you have a medical condition.

Cover design, illustrations and editing by Rachel Orr.

Acknowledgments

I would like to express my gratitude to everyone who contributed to the making of this book by having the courage and open-mindedness to try something different. It has been an inspirational process at every step of the way. Thanks to Rachel Orr for having the gifted vision needed to make it much more than a book, but a beautiful work of art as well. Thanks to my mentors, especially Dr. Effie Chow and Dr. Edgar Mitchell for their encouraging words of wisdom. Thanks to my sister for being herself, and most of all thanks to my Mom and Dad for believing in me.

Adam

Foreword

by Dr. Effie Poy Yew Chow

Hope is a dire need in our present world of turmoil threatened with war, fear, terrorism, and economic downturn. Adam transmits this hope. He is exceptional for his 16 years of age and wise beyond his years and has a special gift for healing. This book portrays the truth on the ultimate healing with love. Everyone, with no exceptions needs to read this book. Each person can learn a great deal from his honest messages. Adam's growth and approach are methodically portrayed and interestingly includes some scientific correlations and analogies.

I have the distinct privilege of being one of Adam's mentors, teachers and friends, so I have closely followed his development with extreme interest. Adam's life has a remarkable balance because not only has Adam become a very talented healer, but also an "A" student in his regular studies in school, and a top ranking athlete in many sports. As well, his family is most loving and supportive. Therefore, the energy that he emanates in his healing is untroubled, pure and fresh.

As part of my own interest, and as an appointee by the President of the United States to the 20 member White House Commission on Complementary and Alternative Medicine Policy (WHCCAMP), I have observed innumerable international healers. Adam is amongst the most gifted ones in his field of healing. In addition, with over 40 years of experience in healing and teaching, one learns to discern the levels of spiritual-ness in healing. Adam reflects a level of honesty and truth that is of the purist form.

There is a serious challenge too in his life. Adam having always had the ability to see and feel energy fields, naturally as though this was a normal everyday occurrence. However, upon revelation that this skill was highly unusual, he had to deal with this immense "difference". The phenomenon of seeing energy fields is known to the community of complementary and Alternative Medicine, but among the general population, it is still misunderstood. Adam, being so young, is taking a courageous stance to be willing to openly discuss his special healing skills and cases in this book. He is in the forefront of helping people understand that there is another dimension in life. He is also willing to subject his fine healing skills to the scrutiny of scientific research especially in the area of cancer and tumours. Adam, I will gladly assist you in making connections to accomplish that noble goal.

Adam is a model of hope, that our youth of today can bring healing and thus peace to this troubled world. His book "DreamHealer" is a must read for everyone to enable all to have courage to be different and respect those who are different. He will enable us to maximize our own human potential to bring about a better world.

Wishing you the greatest success and love, I am honoured to know you, Adam.

Effie Poy Yew Chow
PhD, RN, DiplAc(NCCAOM),
Licensed Acupuncturist in CA, Qigong Grandmaster
President, East West Academy of Healing Arts, San Francisco
www.eastwestqi.com

Table of Contents

THE dREAM IS OUR VISION.

THE DREAM

THE DREAM is a mystical connection with universal energy, which expands life's perspective to a non-ordinary state of consciousness.

We interpret our reality through our five senses: sight, sound, smell, taste and touch. Our awareness is therefore based on very little input if we evaluate it only through those five sensory input areas. With our eyes, we see only a very small part of the electromagnetic spectrum. We hear only a fraction of the known frequency range. And we have no way of quantifying the amount or range perceived from our sense of smell, taste and touch senses.

But we are still bombarded with input whether it is measurable or not. It is fair to assume that we have some awareness of it, and react to it. Therefore it is subjective sensitivity that interprets all of our sensory data. This leaves the door open for the extended human capacity to process information such as intuition, feelings, visions and dreams.

THE dream IS OUR VISION OF PERFECT HEALTH.

THE healer IS OUR GUIDE ALONG THIS PATH.

THIS BOOK PORTRAYS THE truth ON THE ULTIMATE HEALING WITH LOVE.

Dr. Effie Chow

CHAPTER 1

Discovery

TO PERCEIVE beyond OURSELVES IS TO TRULY SEE.

Adam

DISCOVERY

God must have a sense of humor. I don't know how else to explain the irony of my placement on this planet.

I was born into a regular middle class family in a large cosmopolitan city. About 30 percent of the population in the area are of Chinese descent and had I been born into a home within this community, the cultural channels of Qigong or Taoism would embrace my uniqueness. It would be accepted as a rarity, not a weirdness. The main thing is that it would be accepted.

The next largest visible minority is East Indian and if I were born into this culture I could be spirited away to an ashram for mentoring. Again, the culture itself recognizes uncommon talents such as mine as gifts to be honed and developed. They are not only accepted, they are respected.

In contrast, the beliefs and customs of the western culture to which I was assigned do not seem to welcome that which is not common. For some reason it purports to celebrate individualism, in reality what is accepted is sameness. It is a culture that likes everyone to do and be similar. Different is viewed as strange. At best, it is tolerated. What is valued is what we can process with the five senses and nothing beyond them. In the western culture, reality must be measurable.

When I was born, I had a birthmark in the form of a red 'V' on the center of my forehead. I have been told this is the 'Mark of a Healer' because it was located on what is called the third eye. The third eye is where a healer channels their energy to connect with others for healing purposes. The 'V' mark has faded considerably. It can barely be seen now, but it is still vascular because when I become emotional it shows up.

My Great Grandmother on my Mother's side always saw auras (the energy field which surrounds people) and thought that everyone else did. It wasn't until she was around 18 years old that she discovered no one else she knew saw them. At this point she made a conscious decision to turn this off. She still saw them all through her life but did not process the incoming information that her gift provided. She chose to ignore it rather than develop it.

My Dad has North American Indian blood on his mother's side through the Penobscot Indian Nation based in the state of Maine. I have always enjoyed the idea of my native heritage and it's connection with nature and the universal energy. Research has indicated that I am related to the last known tribal shaman healer. His name was Sockalexis.

Although some shaman used their power to do harm to their enemies, Sockalexis was known to only do healings, so he was highly respected and not feared by his fellow tribesmen. A shaman has to be humble and aware of his own strengths and weaknesses in order to help others. He must be able to use his skills and powers to adapt to any situation. This position requires a clear balance of mind, body, heart and spirit. Healing must be an intuitive quest of learning about others and ourselves.

The meeting of these two spiritual worlds from my Mother's side and my Father's side formed my unconscious awareness and unknowingly led me along this path.

"When a man sits down in quietness to listen to the teachings of his spirit, many things will come to him in knowledge and understanding."
- Chief Dan George

Many things that I see are not visible to most people. For example, I see auras. I describe them as the visual life energy that surrounds every living thing. They appear to me as a luminous glow, which I see in various colors and patterns. People, animals and even plants all have auras. They show that the living organism is functioning.

Because of this ability to see auras, I had no trouble distinguishing reality from the fantasy world of television. As a little kid, I remember watching television and telling my Mom and Dad that there were 'real' people and TV people. Auric fields of people and all life are lost in the transmission of television signals, hence people on TV were seen as totally different than real people. That was helpful in determining the difference between real and 'make believe.'

My abilities to see also created some problems for me, as you can imagine. As a kid, Hide 'n Seek was not a game that I enjoyed. Some parents might have worried that because I didn't want to play Hide 'n Seek, perhaps I was antisocial. Or too shy. But that wasn't the case at all. I just couldn't figure out the point of the game. Someone might be hiding behind an object such as a tree, but they would still be visible to me. Their aura would show beyond the tree's outline. It seemed as ludicrous as a large man trying to hide behind a broomstick. I didn't know that others weren't able to see the way I did. That was something I had to learn. Before I did, the point of games such as Hide 'n Seek were a mystery to me.

Every time we went into the wilderness as a family, I would spot wildlife long before others. For me, the auras of the animals were visible through the brush or forest. Many times my family couldn't see what I did as our car traveled along a highway. But often enough, others eventually spotted it too, and my sightings were believed. It is human nature to only believe what we can see. I read a quote once that said, "Vision is the ability to see what isn't there." I see and feel the universal connectedness of all living things — human, animal and plant. I always have. I was born with it.

By the time I was in high school, I had to learn to tone down auras. They were glaringly bright and had become obtrusive. Turning them down had an interesting result for me. As I turned down the visual auras my intuitiveness, or psychic ability increased. In high school I also learned that there were others who saw auras like I did. But we all kept it hidden, from our classmates and even from each other. Accepting and understanding this phenomena was never encouraged.

Many people can see auras or were able to see them at one time in their life. When I look at most babies I can tell that they are very much aware of a person's aura. I can change mine and the baby's eyes will follow the aura as it grows in size or shrinks. This is something that is not nurtured in children mainly out of ignorance of its existence. Some children are even forced to suppress it, as the parents might be fearful of their child being labeled mentally unstable.

A family's religious belief might pose a problem in accepting something like this. The medical community may want to prescribe drugs to 'stop the hallucinations.' The dogma of society has us thinking and believing that it is something that needs fixing.

Back in the 1600s, when people used their special abilities to heal they were often called witches and burnt at the stake. The leaders and scholars of the day would do their best to keep the people ignorant of what was really happening.

They couldn't be further from the truth. Special abilities like mine have to be nurtured and understood, in order to benefit all human kind.

But our thinking has a long way to go.

For now, I know that what I experience is not understood and accepted. Rather, it is generally misunderstood and feared. I learned early in life that a regular kid in tennis shoes and T-shirt had to keep quiet about being different.

Fortunately, my parents are rare and special spirits in that they came to accept my uniqueness. Even more, they came to realize my need for special guidance, or mentoring as it is sometimes called. They had the courage and the wisdom to allow me to be *me*. Within the context of a loving home environment and their open mindedness, I have been allowed to grow and thrive with my gift. For this I will always be grateful. Because of them, I have a better chance of reaching my potential.

It couldn't have been easy for my parents. As I entered my teenage years and telekinetic activities occasionally occurred, I was puzzled. I'm sure my parents were a little more than puzzled as well. Initially, they disbelieved it. Understandably, it was hard for them to accept.

It was especially difficult for my father who would always look for a scientific explanation for everything. It was easier for me because what was happening to me was my normal. I didn't know anything else.

Strange things were always happening to me. Objects would often fly around the room when I went to touch them or pick them up. Sometimes the pencil I was writing with would suddenly have a mind of its own and take off across the room. This happened in school, and I guess everyone figured I must have been throwing them. I let them think that. It was easier than telling them that they were trajected all on their own. I didn't know why or how this was happening. I learned to live with it.

But the first time my bicycle did a 360° spin around while I was riding it, I knew something was really different about me. My Mom was with me when it happened, and she could hardly believe her eyes. I was glad she saw it. It is hard to keep discounting things that you know are true. It's even harder when others keep discounting things you know are true.

Things were always happening to me that didn't happen to anyone else I knew. I tried to hide it from the outside world, and was pretty successful at doing so. But it became impossible to hide from my parents. We did a lot of activities together as a family, so they began to witness enough strange events that even my scientifically minded father could no longer deny it. He saw objects hit the ceiling with great force after I reached out to touch them.

The turning point for him, though, came one day while we were at the gym working out together. A 45-pound barbell fell off its rack near where I was standing and missed my Dad's head by inches. We thought the equipment was faulty so we spent a great deal of time trying to duplicate the event, but to no avail. There was absolutely nothing wrong with the equipment. It was at this point that my Dad finally understood that unexplainable events were truly happening. As I said earlier, it seems to be easier for us to believe what we ourselves have seen.

After that, his attitude changed and he became insatiably curious about my abilities. Now both my parents became focussed on how they could help me develop my gifts. Together, we began a journey.

EACH journey BEGINS WITH A SINGLE STEP.

Adam

Chapter 2

The Journey Begins

WE ARE ALL IN THIS together WORKING
TOWARDS THE GREATER GOOD.

Adam

THE JOURNEY BEGINS

My Dad is the type of guy that you want to have around in an emergency. He's calm, levelheaded and unflappable. He's the one that will take charge in a crisis and step right into action. But Dad became worried and concerned at the onset of accepting what was happening to me. Was this dangerous for me? Was it dangerous for others? There must be answers out there somewhere, but where?

In a panic, my Mom phoned Grandma with an SOS. Under normal circumstances, Grandma's advice was taken. It soon became apparent that this was not a typical childhood situation which she had any experience with. At first, her advice was to call a pediatrician. It didn't take long for all involved to realize that this was not the route to take.

Then Mom remembered a woman she had met years ago. This woman had the ability to see auras and what she called external energy flow. Mom phoned with an urgent request for an appointment. Fresh from my episodes of bike flipping and pencil flying, we went to see her. We had no idea what to expect.

It was great. For the first time I totally connected to someone who could discuss what I had thought everyone could see and feel — energy flow. She showed me various pathways and patterns to redirect my energy in order to achieve different effects and emotions. What I was feeling was visible to her as well as myself.

She explained that my bike flipping occurrences were outbursts of energy, like unintentional static electricity. This occurs when I am not focussed on my energy flow, as I have lots of energy that must be patterned properly. It was a great relief to hear that I could do no harm to others or myself. I think that she was correct, as my bike flipping has not reoccurred since I have begun to direct my energy in other ways.

Mom sat speechless throughout the entire session, as this was all new territory for her. But it was definitely not new for me. I understood with total clarity what was happening. I was finally able to control my energy! This came as a great relief to me as well as my parents. Having another sane adult describe what was happening helped us all understand that this was the normal state for me. Her parting words to my Mom and I were that we should look into Qigong (pronounced chee gong). It is sometimes spelled chi, which means energy or life force. Gong is discipline or work.

"With the amount of energy he has, he could be a Grandmaster in a week," she told my parents. I've since learned that it often takes decades of dedicated study to achieve that level.

As suggested, I contacted a Qigong Master in town and made an appointment to see him. It was very interesting to watch as he demonstrated emitting chi (pronounced chee), or energy, which was streaming out of his body through his fingertips. What an experience it was to be able to see this! He had a very large, golden aura that looked like it flowed harmoniously. I was curious and wanted to learn more about energy systems.

This encounter was a turning point for me. I had discovered that I could control and focus my energy. I wasn't flirting with madness, but rather exploring a gift that others shared. From here, I embarked on the self-discovery part of my journey.

Healing Discovery

Two days after this, my Mom was in severe pain with a multiple sclerosis (MS) symptom. MS is a chronic neurological disorder. The symptom is called trigeminal neuralgia, which is a stabbing pain in the face and ear. She had been diagnosed with MS when I was very young, so this was not a new experience for any of us in the family.

That particular night my Dad, my sister and I were watching television and Mom was upstairs in her bedroom smothering her screams in her pillow. The pain that night was, as it was on many nights, unbearable. I went up to her room.

"Close your eyes, Mom," I said to her as I put my hands on her head. Why I did this, I really don't know. It's like I knew what to do. At any rate, she complied and I felt the pain leave her body and enter mine. It was a horrible pain.

I went to my bed and collapsed with a throbbing headache. My Mom drifted off to sleep, as she was then pain free. She has improved a great deal since then and is now able to participate in our family life.

This was a turning point for me in understanding my gifts. It sealed my journey toward healing. As everything seems to evolve for a reason, my Mom's illness was no exception. This was no coincidence, but rather a signpost in my life. It allowed me to start my healing journey from a point of no fear, only with the intention of helping my Mom.

If it weren't for my Mom's illness I likely wouldn't have dived headfirst into healing until years later. Seeing someone whom I love suffer was the inspiration I needed to react without thoughts of whether I could or couldn't help, or of whether this was even possible or not. As if on autopilot, I did what I could do and made another self-discovery — I could heal!!!.

But another challenge emerged for us: I had absorbed her pain and taken it on as my own. Once again my parents were concerned. They certainly didn't want me healing if I was going to be ill myself as a result. Regardless I was instinctively drawn to healing.

I recall sitting in the doctor's office with my Dad and four other kids sitting across from us. While I was waiting my turn, I diagnosed the four children sitting across from me. Of course they were unaware of what I was doing. It made me upset that I couldn't say anything about a baby's condition, as they are verbally unable to express their symptoms. However I could clearly see where the problem was. While driving past bus stops with my parents I always noted injuries and medical conditions of people we passed. Healing and health became a predominant theme in my life.

Initially, I did some treatments on people at my Dad's workplace. They were socially separate from any of my high school friends or neighbors, so I didn't feel threatened if they knew of my unusual abilities. During this period of time I learned a lot just by practicing.

My parents were still not confident enough to be relaxed about my healing experiences. They wondered about the possibilities of me picking up some serious disease, as I was learning and practicing new techniques. After many sleepless nights, they called Dr. Effie Chow, a Qigong Grandmaster.

Mom met Dr. Chow years earlier at a Qigong demonstration. Dr. Chow is founder and president of the East West Academy of Healing Arts (EWAHA). In July 2000, President Clinton appointed Dr. Chow to the original 15 member White House Commission on Complementary and Alternative Medicine Policy. Dr. Chow has a Ph.D. in higher education and a master's degree in behavioral sciences and communication. She is a registered public health and psychiatric nurse and Qigong Grandmaster with 35 years experience. She is a National Diplomat (NCCAOM) and a California-licensed acupuncturist since 1977.

Even with her qualifications and busy schedule, she managed to find time to come to our city and mentor me for three days. The time with her was very valuable and played a major role in pointing me in the right direction. She told me about important things like grounding and effectively separating good and bad energies. Most of all, she helped my parents stop worrying about my unusual abilities. She taught us to accept them for what they are, and to understand that it is a gift. She also gave us little gems that we will always remember.

One that stands out is that "we all need at least three belly aching laughs a day." I have the ability to heal someone, but it is up to him/her to stay well. They must be able to enjoy life and maintain a sense of humor. Laughter has been proven to help people heal and stay well. Whether it is a chemical being secreted in the body, or simply the idea of having fun, it works.

Dr. Chow has given me guidance in so many other ways in the healing arts and I am very grateful to her. It was a breath of fresh air to talk with someone who was experienced in energy healing. When my Dad and I attended one of her workshops, she carried out amazing energy demonstrations, which were very helpful.

These experiments further demonstrated how inter-connected we really are. Changing the energy field of one person would affect all persons in or near that energy field. If someone is in a negative mood then all people around him/her will have a tendency to feel negative. Of course, the reverse works as well. If you are around someone who is positive, then you will tend to be in a positive mood.

One of the most important things I learned from Dr. Chow was visualization. When I first met her, I had limited experience in removing energy blockages from people. With a bit of information on how to visualize different tools for removing energy blocks, I was able to be more effective with my healings.

For example, when I first looked at someone with multiple sclerosis, the disease looked to me like grains of green sand. My normal approach was to envision picking each grain up and throwing it away. I found this technique extremely inefficient as the blockages would return as fast as I could remove them. Dr. Chow showed me a more effi-cient visualization method which made my healing much simpler.

Some day in the future, being able to heal by thought will be the norm. Perhaps I can help facilitate motion in that direction. I hope so.

CHAPTER 3

Finding

My Way

EVERY PERSON IS BORN WITH
GIFTS. LIFE ITSELF IS THE MOST
precious OF THEM.

Adam

Finding My Way

A journey is a sequence of events. It begins with the first step, which in my case was the recognition that I was somehow different. I believe it is the responsibility of all of us to use the gifts with which we are born. I choose to use mine for the benefit of others. It would be a shame to ignore it and deprive others of this knowledge and benefit.

Every person is born with gifts. Life itself is the most precious of them. Life gives one the connection to what I call the universal energy system. The science of quantum physics refers to this as the field of quantum information. Awareness of this connection is in itself a gift.

People's gifts and talents vary. My younger sister has the gift of a musical ear. Wherever she goes she hears music. Whether she is in a shopping mall or in the wilderness she is tuned into it. She can't ignore it or turn it off. It is one of her gifts.

Visual artists must see a potential painting everywhere they look. Along the highway at viewpoints they are seen with easels, trying to capture the beauty of the moment in a two dimensional impression for later enjoyment.

It may take an artist to see the emerging work of art, but everyone can appreciate the incredible beauty of a rock faced deep canyon with the river below roaring toward to the open ocean. Evergreens line the edges and their scent permeates our thought into a timeless wonderment. Gusts of strong winds energize us as we feel our connectedness to the universal energy system, which engulfs us, connects us and is us. We can feel the oneness with all, and artists try to capture that feeling with their gifts.

Others are gifted with minds that can problem-solve. Some have the gift of legal comprehension, and they spend their lives defending others that need it. Some people have charisma and inspire others to be their best. All gifts are important. We are interdependent on each other's contributions. As such, no gift is any more, nor any less, important than any other gift.

One of my gifts is being sensitive to our connected-ness with the universal energy and each other. It goes by many names. But whatever it is called, it is a connection which we all share, hence the universal energy system. Calling it that is more straightforward than "May the force be with you," as the force is always with you (and every-one else for that matter). Some people are aware of it, and others are not, but it is there nonetheless.

There are so many things that happen in life that one passes off as just a coincidence. From some of my experi-ences, I have begun to think differently on this topic.

Have you ever heard yourself say, "I *knew* that was going to happen"? Many of us have had that experience. Something happens, and when it does, we have the feeling that we just *knew* what was going to occur. We receive information from the universal information grid constantly. It is just a matter of screening out what you don't need and making sense of what is useful. We must be aware of these coincidences and cultivate their messages and meaning.

Most coincidences are messages being sent for a rea-son and that reason may have to do with you. It might be intended for someone with whom you will be in contact. Perhaps you are being used as a conduit for another person in need.

All information past and present is still out there and available to us. Universal energy field means exactly that - universal. All inventions, medical cures, and knowledge come from the universal energy system.

Sometimes we access great ideas and surprise ourselves. Now, the human ego being what it is, one might be tempted to assume that they are very smart to have come up with the idea. There is nothing wrong with thinking good about yourself. But the fact of the matter is that you did not come upon this great idea solely through your own thought. You were assisted by many people who have their ideas filed in the universal energy field. We all share our thoughts and ideas in this way.

And sometimes, it is accessed simultaneously. The refrigerator, for example, was invented at the same time by two different men in two different countries. They were never in touch with each other, but each accessed the needed information at the same time.

A friend of my Mom's is a great designer and many of her clients and associates are in awe of her work. Frequently they ask her how she comes up with such unique and amazing designs and some people are quite disappointed when she does not claim the glory.

"I honestly don't know how I am able to create these results," she always says. "But I don't feel like they come *from* me. It feels like they come *through* me."

I know what she means, and I appreciate her awareness. But it is often hard for those around her to accept it. They think that maybe she has a self-esteem problem, or something. I don't. She is simply aware of her connection to the universal energy system and routinely taps into it during her creative processes. I tap into the universal energy system to do my healing.

Healing is something that I can't ignore. This ability is not coincidental. It was given to me for a reason and I plan to use it. I still go to high school and do regular social and sport activities. However, being able to remove illness from people is very rewarding. I just wish that I had more time to treat everyone who needs it, as well as play basketball, tennis, snowboard, chat with my girlfriend and just generally hang out with my friends. I am a regular 16-year-old...sort of.

Because of my gift of sensitivity to the universal connectedness, I am able to heal. I think I always knew I could heal, but thought that I needed to hide the ability from others. I'd be alienated, and/or rejected if I exposed this to people around me. Many others who have unusual abilities feel they must choose between a social life or living with this uniqueness. I choose both. My social life is important to me. But so is the ability to share my healing gifts, so I must somehow find a way to integrate both.

I have had the privilege of being tutored by some truly amazing people. They know who they are, and I want to thank them for all their help and support as I continue to make my way in this world.

When I first began healing, I found it very draining. Sometimes, painful and exhausting because I took the other person's pain. But like everything else, practice makes perfect.

One of the things I had to learn was to do what I do, in a way that didn't harm me. That was important to my ever-vigilant parents. My Mom is especially watchful that I do not overextend myself and that I get enough rest. This meant I had to find a way to heal without taking on the other person's pain. So with some coaching from experts in the healing arts, and over time, I fine-tuned and developed my own techniques. As it turned out, there was much I was going to learn.

My first step was to know that seeing external auras or human energy fields is rare, but certainly not unique to me. I had thought that everyone sees what I do. I soon realized that this is a gift and I learned that I can control it. It can also be redirected and connected with any other life energy field, including all humans, animals and plant life. This energy field connection could be used for the purpose of healing. Many times I felt I was in uncharted territory as I explored this new gift. I have developed my own methods and style of healing through self-teaching. But that is not to say that I have not had input along the way.

The energy healing I do is not Reiki (Japanese healing art), Qigong, touch therapy or faith healing. It falls under no particular discipline. My ability to heal is what comes naturally to me. I wanted to learn what other healers do so I have met with many of them. With my ability to see auras it is obvious to me what is happening as I can see the energy flow from healer to patient. What is apparently invisible to most people, including many healers, is clearly visible to me.

One of the first healers I saw showed me how to ground my energy. Grounding is connecting one's life energy to Earth's energy. He explained that with exhaling, I should imagine the flow of my energy traveling down my body, through the soles of my feet all the way to the center of the Earth. This knowledge of grounding energy is essential to everyone. With each inhale, we connect to the universal energy system by breathing in, and absorbing it. This completes the energy circuit, and we ground. I was thrilled with this knowledge and now my energy flows smoothly.

Another mentor I saw is a Reiki psychic healer and I learned something of this type of healing. I engaged in telepathic communication or mind talk with this person. To be able to knowingly do this with another person was a first for me. We would sit in the same room and have conversations without any verbal words being exchanged. Instead, communication happened with an exchange of images. I enjoyed this form of communication, as it is so efficient compared to verbal communication.

Later I met another healer who also communicated in images with me. He had cured himself of terminal cancer and is now world famous for helping others. He works by increasing the vibrational level of the body. From him I learned about the vibrational levels of various colors and how this affects healing. Our bodies are tuned into so many more aspects of the universe than we give ourselves credit for.

I also had the pleasure of meeting a famous healer who discovered his healing ability quite by accident. He spent most of his life working in a high tech field, while trying to avoid his connection. Of course, he found that he had to use this gift. It would wait until he was ready to use it, but it would not go away.

I found that each healer's strengths are different and I have incorporated into my healings a technique or idea from most that I have met. From all, I learned something very valuable: we are all in this together working towards the greater good. It will take the devotion of many to awaken mankind to our connectivity.

My vision goes much deeper than the exterior aura of energy, which surrounds all living things. I have the ability to see energy fields, at many different frequencies, which enables me to do a type of body scan on a person. Dr. Effie Chow, in her book *Miracle Healing from China*, mentions this as a rare ability of a few Qigong Masters.

It wasn't long after I discovered this that I found that all I needed was a photograph of someone to be able to see their body scan remotely. This is the technique I use when doing distant healings. It enables me to treat anyone anywhere in the world. The space between us does not matter. A connection is made using this universal stream of information so I don't need to physically be near someone to heal them. Distance is not a factor. Whether the person is on the same continent as I am or not, makes no difference.

This is the point where some knowledge of quantum physics and the quantum hologram are essential to make this leap from our usual material world. The science behind holograms and quantum physics will be explored in more detail in a later chapter.

Initially, I met people engaged in the healing arts who focus on the outer energy area of a person's body, or their aura. Healers use their hands and minds to 'smooth' and repair the energy blockages negatively affecting the body. Many healers have found this to be an effective technique for dealing with health problems.

Auras are an easy place to first notice illness or injury as they are extensions and reflections of the physical body. Illness or injury prominently shows in one's energy field thus leading the healer to the location of the problem. Various colors given out by this energy within the auric field provide lots of information.

The color is not the only visible indicator of trouble. I find that the entire area of the injured or diseased part of the body's aura is disturbed. In other healthier areas of the body, the aura moves and swirls with a pattern or an appearance of harmony and organization. There is a flow. In an afflicted area, this is broken. The appearance is definitely that of disharmony.

It is possible for me to see these blockages or disruptions before the person physically feels it, if it is a new blockage in the body. When it is new, the area may not have been disturbed long enough to cause pain or a noticeable problem. It can be an early warning of a developing problem. This may warrant a preemptive type of treatment. With disease, the earlier it is detected, the easier the problem is to fix. Sound familiar?

IT WILL TAKE THE DEVOTION OF MANY TO Awaken MANKIND TO OUR CONNECTIVITY.

Adam

CHAPTER 4

The Science
Behind It All

ADAM IS A GIFTED AND DEVOTED YOUNG HEALER. HIS WORDS SHOULD BE AN INSPIRATION TO MANY.

Edgar Mitchell, Sc. D.
Founder, Institute of Noetic Sciences.
Apollo Astronaut & Sixth Man to Walk on Moon

The Science Behind It All

My Dad has always taught me that there has to be a scientific explanation for everything. Anything that we can't explain within our existing scientific knowledge base is called a mystery. If something good takes place and we can't explain how it happened, we call it a miracle. This is quite evident throughout our society. Doctors sometimes have patients whom they predict will only live for a few months and to their surprise some patients go on to live for years. The doctors will refer to this as a miracle simply because the understanding of what took place goes beyond their medical training.

Most of the past pioneers of science have been ridiculed for delving into that which does not fall into the scientific views of the day. I have had the honor of meeting a modern day scientist who has no fear to explore what he strongly believes. His name is Dr. Edgar Mitchell.

His name will no doubt be familiar to many readers. On January 31, 1971, Apollo 14 lifted off from Cape Kennedy and three days later, Edgar Mitchell and Alan Shepard walked on the lunar surface. As could be expected from such a dramatic and meaningful experience, Dr. Mitchell's perspective on life and human consciousness would never be the same. A graduate of MIT with a doctorate in aeronautics and astronautics, he has since constructed a theory that could explain not only the mystery of human consciousness, but the psychic event as well, which is something the spiritualist refers to as a miracle and the scientist dismisses altogether. It is my opinion that Dr. Mitchell is one of the great thinkers of our time.

On Dr. Mitchell's return journey to Earth from the moon, he became aware of a deep sense of universal connectedness. This overwhelming awareness would set the course for him in years to come. For more than the next 30 years he would continue to study the mysteries of consciousness and being.

For years Dr. Edgar Mitchell has studied the quantum hologram which puts an important scientific description to human phenomena, including consciousness itself. The scientific papers he has written are complex and go beyond what I would like to cover in this book. His ability to explain things to me in scientific terms has helped me understand my gift and progress with it.

Magic, miracles and natural phenomenon are names we give to things we don't understand with our existing knowledge base. When someone refers to any healing that I do as a miracle, I have to correct them. Everything I do has a scientific basis to it. Dr. Edgar Mitchell is one scientist who has worked with these issues for many years.

His paper entitled *Nature's Mind - The Quantum Hologram*, comes closest to explaining what is happening when I connect to someone's energy field. My view is that there is a scientific explanation for everything, we just have to discover it. It is always a breath of fresh air to come back to Dr. Mitchell for an explanation regarding any changes in my power. He has been very gracious and patient while helping me with my journey through this unusual time in my life. His mentoring has been invaluable to my understanding of the scientific meaning behind my ability.

There is no such thing as random coincidences. Things happen for a reason and I feel that me meeting Dr. Mitchell was an essential part of my development. The chain of coincidences started with my uncle, whose primary hobby has always been manned space travel. His house is full of model rockets and spacecraft. He also has most books written by astronauts including Dr. Edgar Mitchell's book — *The Way of the Explorer*.

My uncle came to our house one day with a pamphlet about a conference entitled *Quickening Global Consciousness*. This was the first time I heard about IONS (Institute of Noetic Sciences), the organization which Dr. Mitchell founded 30 years ago. Among many other issues, it explores distant healing.

This information came to me at the exact moment in time that I needed it. Had this happened even a month before, I don't think that I would have been ready for it. On the day of the conference my parents and I arrived early and got a seat near the front. There were two extra chairs at our table in a room with 200 people in the audience and several empty tables at the back.

Just before the guest speaker was introduced, a close personal friend of Dr. Mitchell's joined us. We, of course, didn't realize the connection until we began chatting during the intermission. Although I didn't want to reveal why I had come (I was still uncomfortable with people knowing about my healing gift) it was impossible NOT to mention it. Dr. Mitchell's friend had recently been in a car accident and was interested in me seeing the injuries and treating them. She was so taken by my healing abilities that she decided to introduce us to Dr. Mitchell.

Since then I have appreciated the basic knowledge, guidance and insight that Dr. Mitchell and the IONs organization has offered me. It is very settling to meet intelligent people who want to explore and understand the unknown. The world would never have advanced to where it is today if it weren't for people like Dr. Edgar Mitchell.

And people like physicist Max Planck. Just over 100 years ago, Mr. Planck wrote a mathematical formula that introduced the world to the concept of tiny bundles of energy that behave both as waves and as particles. They came to be known as quanta. His formula became the basis of quantum physics, and gave birth to a branch of science where reality does not follow the cause-and-effect rules of our ordinary empirical science. This changed our most basic concept of our physical world.

Humans do not welcome change. There is great resistance to it in all aspects of life. Mainstream science was shocked when the idea was first proposed that the world is round, not flat. Scientists were determined to reject the concept.

Indeed, the "Flat Earth Society" was adamant that anyone who believed the world was round had lost their mind. Within the scholar community, it didn't matter whether you asked one of them or ten of them, you would get the same response. They all shared the same thought, theory and answers. Hundreds of years later, we readily accept that the earth is round, and think that those who fought so hard to hold on to the belief and doctrine that the world was flat were out of *their* minds.

It is common for new concepts to initially be viewed with suspicion. It is true of any science of the day, including medical science. Whether you ask one or ten doctors the same question, the answer comes out of the same body of knowledge for the time period. In our present age, doctors use knives, radiation, and toxic drugs to treat cancer and everything else. Over time, many of these treatments and procedures will be superceded. I am fortunate in that I am not restricted by the dogma of the day as to what is possible or impossible.

I have found that understanding some of the basics of quantum theory is necessary to explain how distant healing is possible. In the quantum world, the nature of reality is said to embrace the following concepts:

1. A quantum object (for example an electron) can be at more than one place at a time.

2. A quantum object cannot be said to manifest in ordinary space-time reality until we observe it as a particle.

3. A quantum object ceases to exist here, and simultaneously appears in existence over there; we cannot say it went through the intervening space (the quantum leap).

4. A manifestation of one quantum object caused by our observation, simultaneously influences its correlated twin object, no matter how far apart they are (quantum action-at-a-distance). This is also referred to as non-locality.

Courtesy of theoretical physicist Amit Goswami as published on the noetic.org website.

All particles are fundamentally connected to all other particles. All information and knowledge is available in the field of quantum information. Every physical object emits its own quantum hologram, or image whether it is on this planet or on a planet located on the other side of the universe. My visual perception of the field of quantum information looks amazingly similar to what I see in a person's brain. When I see the inside of the brain at an energetic level, I see synapses clicking on and off at an astonishing rate through a network of pathways which connect every neuron in the brain.

Each node in the field of quantum information I am viewing is a bright dense light that looks a bit like a spider cocoon. Each cocoon has zillions of pathways that stretch out, each attaching to another cocoon. This pattern seems to continue to infinity.

The following words from the Vedas of ancient India are apparently over 7000 years old. They came to me from a friend and I think they are great words. I think they are great words. It is interesting to me how they match my visualization of the universal energy system, or field of quantum information.

Indra's Net
There is an endless net of threads throughout
the universe.
The horizontal threads are in space.
The vertical threads in time.
At every crossing of threads there is an individual.
And every individual is a crystal bead.
The great light of absolute being illuminates and
penetrates every crystal being,

And every crystal being reflects not only the light from
every other crystal in the net,
But also every reflection of every re-flection throughout
the universe.

A person who is intuitive and energetically powerful can access this field and query it to find any information ever available. When an intuitive individual connects to another person, the information is received instantaneously because of this interconnectedness. Indra's Net puts this complex concept into very simple and timeless words.

The most important part of the quantum hologram that relates to my healing gift is that quantum attribute of nature called non-locality. At the quantum level, action on two particles, which are part of a single system, occur instantaneously at a distance. It doesn't matter how far apart they appear to be. This gives me a better understanding how I am able to heal someone through distant healing. I connect to a person's quantum hologram, which is a non-local information mechanism. I am then able to give information to the person's body through intentionality, which causes the body to change. The person's new state of wellness will then be emitted in the quantum hologram. With my intent to heal and the person's desire to get better, this can turn into real positive results. I will go into more detail with this in the section of the book, "How I Heal."

In the last century, the early adapters of the quantum principles have produced some advanced technologies such as lasers, transistors, and CAT scans. But in many areas, including our everyday lives, it is still very difficult for most people to overlay the quantum phenomena. When we go to work each day, we like to know that our office is exactly where it was when we left yesterday. It would be difficult for architects and engineers who are busy designing and building bridges and skyscrapers to think in terms of something existing in two places at once! It is not an easy reach, to say the least. But, I believe that over time, we will unravel the mysteries of this most interesting form of science and learn to apply the principles and concepts into many areas that will benefit us enormously.

How I Heal

I have been asked many times what I see, experience and know, when I do a healing. When I first started healing, the person would be seated next to me while my arm and hand would be outstretched toward them. This would enable my energy system to interact with theirs. Now distance is not a barrier. It makes no difference if the other person is sitting next to me or on the other side of the world.

When I see a photograph of the person, I can instantly connect to their energy system.

During a treatment, I project holographic images, or holograms in front of me. Holograms are the visual guidance or three-dimensional maps, which appear before me when I am viewing someone for treatment. All of the body's information is available in this manner. Every physical object emits it's own quantum hologram, which contains all information about it. From this field of quantum information, I can focus or zoom in using specific information or views, which I project as a hologram.

When I go into someone, I can effectively tune-in to various subsets of information. It's kind of like changing channels on the TV. My mind acts as the remote control, which adjusts to a different set of frequencies, thus giving me a different holographic view. I have named each hologram that I use for healing.

Once this hologram appears I can manipulate the energy so that the person can find their way back to a healthy state. People who have observed me doing this tell me that it looks as though I am conducting an orchestra. My arms and hands wave through the air, and my fingers nimbly create patterns as I make energy adjustments. It appears to the observer to be mesmerizing yet patterned flowing gestures, like the dancing of flames in a raging fire. Through intentions of healing, I provide information to the person I am treating. I do this by being in resonance with the person's body.

In this way the body of the person is interacting and exchanging information with me. This then stimulates the person to energetically alter their state of wellness, which is in turn reflected in their hologram. I can usually see this change starting to take place immediately.

Everyone's body knows it's own way back to wellness, it just needs some guidance. These specific adjustments to their energy system help them to achieve this. I have done this hundreds of times, yet my parents always want to watch. Mom says that she can feel it every time I do it.

As I developed and practiced my techniques, I found a way where instead of *taking on* the pain of the person I was treating, I was able to *dispose* of it. I send it to a place kind of like a black hole. I don't destroy it; it seems to die on its own without the host organism (the person's body).

Many times now, I feel more energy after I've treated someone. But I had to learn to use *their* energy to do the treatment rather than mine. It really is better that way anyway, as I have also learned that all healing is really done by the person themselves. I know this might sound a bit confusing, but it is true. I will explain more as we go along in this book. Since then I have discovered that using the universal energy source is a far more efficient and powerful method of healing. This seemingly endless source of energy is much more efficient to use than using a person's own energy to heal.

LEARNING can only be done by oneself.
NOBODY ELSE can learn anything FOR us.
HEALING can only be accomplished by oneself.
NOBODY ELSE can heal FOR us.
TEACHERS can mentor us, direct us to information,
Encourage and assist us in the process.
HEALERS can help us to connect to our own energy
sources, give us hope and guidance.
When we are ready we will LEARN the knowledge
ourselves.
When we are ready we will HEAL our bodies ourselves.
Our minds will LEARN, and
Our bodies will HEAL
Only when we are ready.

LEARNING CAN ONLY BE
DONE BY ONESELF.

CHAPTER 5

Holograms

&

Colors

THROUGH MY intentions TO HEAL, I
CAN GIVE NEW INFORMATION TO
THAT PERSON'S BODY, WHICH
ALLOWS IT TO CHANGE TO ITS NEW
STATE OF HEALTH.

Adam

Holograms & Colors

Using Holograms

Healing started for me by using the overall energy hologram, which shows energy blockages. I am constantly evolving new techniques and holographic layers for the new challenges I meet in healing. Presently, I use at least 8 holographic projections, which I refer to as holograms, and by the time this book is finished I'm sure I will be using more. Every hologram is useful for different conditions and situations.

When I first started healing, I saw and worked with one hologram to see, identify and clear energy blockages. I could do a virtual tour of the inside of one's body with what appeared to me like a still photo of all the organs and inner structure of the body. Energy blockages appeared prominently in the foreground so I was able to easily see and remove them. I often found this work tiring and sometimes had a headache afterwards. When I am working with a hologram I lose all sense of time. I also had to be very careful to remember to breathe rather than hold my breath. This now comes very naturally to me but it was certainly part of the learning process to get comfortable with doing this. I definitely had much to discover about my techniques.

One day I was looking at a young man with a heart problem. All of a sudden and unintentionally, I found myself inside his body in live time! I was totally surrounded by the beating heart, pulsating blood, contracting arteries and moving valves!

I couldn't escape this overwhelming realistic view. Graphic images surrounded me. I stepped back in awe and total shock of what I was experiencing. Believe me, it wasn't a pretty sight. I released myself during my step backwards and once out I felt ill, dizzy and exhausted. I immediately had to go to bed and sleep it off.

Since that experience, I have learned how to go in and out of this holographic view of ones body without getting grossed out. Now I can control this rather than it controlling me.

I have a total sense of being there, and I can watch the entire body in action from the inside. I take a *visual tour* of the body of the person I am treating *from the inside*. I can see every organ as it is functioning, or struggling to function. I see and hear the heart pumping. I watch cancer grow. I watch the traffic of synapses in the brain. Every cell and every activity can be visible to me as I go through the treatment. I call it going in. I don't do this all the time. Usually I go into the energetic hologram and only do the physical real-time hologram if it is needed for a specific problem.

Using the information available to everyone in the field of quantum information, I tune into subsets of information for healing. Just as a person turns the dial on a receiver to change frequencies, I am able to do this adjustment within my mind. I can then project this subset of information as a holographic image in front of me. I have found through experience that certain holograms received are more useful for different ailments. As if I am using a microscope, I am able to zoom in and out as required. Through my intentions to heal, I can then give new information to that person's body, which allows it to change to its new state of health. The following are the holographic views which I use most frequently.

1. Energetic Hologram

This is the first hologram that I learned to use. It is the most basic level and for many simple ailments it is the most effective. I can see the overall view of the energetic body. The body's energy system grid shows the flow of energy, as well as any blockages, old or new. This can also indicate whether a problem may arise if the body is left untreated. Energy changes provide a grid-type guide for the person's physical body to model for their path to healing.

If something is removed on the energetic level, then it will soon disappear on the physical level. A woman I treated had been bleeding vaginally and had gone to see her gynecologist before seeing me. He ordered an ultrasound of her uterus, and a fibroid mass (polyp) was found. Surgery was scheduled to remove it.

I went in and had no trouble locating the bleeding area. It was a very small mass that was causing the problem. I energetically removed it and saw that her body was adjusting to the change. In her hologram it looked as if her body would continue to heal itself. Six weeks later when the surgery was performed, the gynecologist was amazed to find that there was no fibroid present. He told the woman that he didn't understand this but if it reoccurs it is something unrelated as "this case is closed."

2. Brain Signals Hologram

I can see the flow of electrical impulses along neurons and intuitively know their function. I can see damaged connections in this hologram, which are specific to certain brain functions. All of the switches in the brain allow (or prevent) the passage of electrical impulses. The flow and blockages of these electrical pathways form a specialized holographic view of the brain. This is a very useful tool for headaches, migraines and neurological disorders. Some recurring problems need the brain to be reset in order to correct a condition.

A woman I know was misdiagnosed as having MS many years ago, before the newest diagnostic tests were available. Recently, she had an MRI and as a result was told that she does NOT have MS. Instead, she was informed that her cerebellum just stopped functioning. She had great difficulty with mobility and used a walker, which had contributed to the MS misdiagnosis. The neurologist could not establish what caused her condition, but it did not appear to be progressive in nature.

When I first went in, I could see right away that part of her brain had no functioning neurons. I used her Brain Signals Hologram to get the flow of energy going in this area. After a few sessions I could see an energetic difference as new pathways were developing. However, she felt nothing, and thanked me for my efforts.

I heard from her several months after our sessions. She noticed a gradual but marked improvement in her mobility and coordination. The physical improvement DID follow these energetic strides that I saw. It just took more time to react than with most conditions.

Viewing the brain signals hologram in real-time is like being in the middle of a 3D superhighway. There are electrical impulses flying along pathways everywhere, and I do mean flying. The speed at which they travel is incredible. It takes some practice to feel comfortable viewing this hologram.

3. Real-time Physical Hologram

The real-time physical hologram includes the skeletal, nerve, blood, lymph, and organ systems. I can see any of these at a cellular level, if needed, and adjust them to their best healing potential. I like to use this hologram to observe the functioning of different body systems. From here, I can determine the next course of action.

This hologram is very useful when the person I am treating has been diagnosed with diseases such as fibromyalgia and rheumatoid arthritis. Physical problems are usually corrected more directly and efficiently using this hologram.

4. Smart Energy Packets

Through intentionality I send these pac-man like units into the body's information to reduce the unwanted blockages and replace them with good energy. At first, I called them energy cutter bugs, but too many people reacted to this name. I guess no one wants to imagine 'bugs' in their system. So now I call them 'smart energy packets' (SEPs), which is actually more accurate.

SEPs are an extremely useful healing tool for me. For example, they can continue to heal long after my treatment is finished. It is a tool that I use to eliminate things on an energetic level that would require ongoing work. I use these on infections, cancer and anything where problems are likely to reoccur.

They are more than a 'seek and destroy' device as they have a sack on them that spreads good healing energy in their path. They can also reproduce themselves and communicate with each other. This ability is useful, as they can send signals to each other to 'shock' or 'jump-start' the system. I am constantly developing new SEP's that are more efficient and effective.

5. Pattern Energy Grid

The pattern of the energy grid can reveal if there is a dysfunction or disease, which will occur because the source of it stubbornly remains. When you look at 3D contour maps, you can quickly tell if there is an imperfection in the graph. This is similar to how I detect dysfunction or disease in the pattern energy grid. There is harmony and flow in a healthy system, and a disruption is easily visible around the dysfunction when I view this hologram. Old stubborn injuries appear very prominently in this hologram. New injuries are not as pronounced. This view is NOT of the external aura, but is a view of much deeper energy patterns within the body.

6. Heat

I have found this is a hologram which is necessary in the treatment of cancer. To me, cancer cells appear as green before treatment. After red heat is energetically applied, they gradually go white and disintegrate like dust. I energetically vacuum up the dead pieces to get rid of the dead material.

This energetic heat, or high frequency energy, is useful for cancer because it pops cancer cells from the inside out. They explode on the energetic level and die. If something is dead on the energetic level, then it usually dies shortly thereafter in the physical level.

7. Genetic

This is my latest holographic image that I use during a treatment. I know there are many applications within the information contained in this hologram. I will continue researching it so I can fully understand its potential.

Genetically based diseases are complicated as the body envisions the defect as its rightful and healthy state. You and I might think of it as a defect, but in genetically based diseases, the body thinks that it is the correct way to be. Because it is so complex, I don't use this view currently.

8. Overall View Hologram

I compare how this hologram looks before and after every treatment to see if the person has accepted the new pattern of health. It should then appear obvious to me that energy blockages have been removed. Some people and some conditions appear to shift toward health in one treatment. Others take more treatments and time. This overall view is how I know whether more treatments are needed. The effectiveness of a treatment varies with each individual.

Using Colors

Colors have different energy frequencies. They are applicable to any hologram for healing. I realize that there have been many suggestions as to what each color 'means' and how it can be used for manipulating moods and even healing. I have simply observed colors, their vibrations and their effects. Over time, I have figured out how they work by watching auras and studying energy fields. I watch how auras look and move when people are sick and when they are not. That is how I have come to know which color to use, and when.

I use many colors which are beyond our visible spectrum, and I can only see them in my mind. Many of these are extremely useful in healing. These colors are impossible to describe. It's like asking someone who only sees the color green to describe the color red.

I have been asked if the average person can help themselves (or someone else) by visualizing the appropriate color around them, or around the afflicted area. My answer is that it depends on the person. Most people, who are willing to discipline themselves and learn to focus, can use colors to help themselves and others. Everyone has the ability to heal to some degree. The section of this book entitled "Seven Steps for Life" outlines how everyone can maximize this capability.

If you break anything in the universe down to its very basics, you have energy. Light is energy which we can see in a frequency range of 380 THz to 770 THz (THZ is terahertz 10^12). If we are exposed to large doses of electromagnetic waves in the upper frequencies like ultraviolet, X-rays, gamma rays or cosmic rays, we will eventually die from this exposure. It should be no surprise that cancer will also die from exposure to high frequency electromagnetic waves. This has been proven and is used in a number of medical technologies to kill cancer. The problem is that this often kills normal cells which surround the cancer, causing serious side effects.

One of the methods I use to treat diseases is to apply high energy directly to the diseased area without damaging normal cells. The only side effect is from the body adjusting to a new, and consequently unfamiliar, healthy state. I see the energy that I apply in the form of colors inside the body. During this process I am able to access colors outside the regular color spectrum, which are a much higher frequency and are very useful in healing.

The concentration of a certain color of light is made denser when focused like a laser beam. This makes it more effective for healing small areas. There are so many combinations of colors and densities that it is impossible to summarize all the different results at this stage in my discovery. The following are brief descriptions of some of the colors that I use most frequently.

Color: Yellow

Uses: Yellow is used when a specific organ or localized area requires treatment. It is used to increase energy when someone suffers from a lack of it. Yellow encourages the growth of good energy, and will rejuvenate a person's energy system.

Color: White

Uses: White is used in similar situations as yellow in giving energy. It boosts ones own energy system to fight off the bad energy by joining forces with the immune system.

Color: Purple

Uses: Purple works somewhat the same as SEPs. It attaches like glue to bad energy as if it is sticky. It floats around until it finds bad energy to attach to, then penetrates and eliminates it from the inside out.

Color: Red

Uses: Red is used as a healing color in the heat hologram. It is very useful in the energetic treatment of cancer. Red can be used as a glue, which holds the areas to be healed in place. This enables me to then use the other healing colors to treat the area.

Color: Blue

Uses: Blue is most effective in the form of positive thought. It is 'positive thought in liquid energy form.' Blue prepares the body to be receptive to the healing intentionalities, thereby overshadowing any negative mind/body connections which may exist.

Combinations of colors often work well together, and some are synergistic. White and purple, for example, work well together. But purple is one of, if not THE most difficult color to work with. Using purple takes tremendous focus and concentration, and if not properly applied, it will simply dissipate.

I DON'T NEED TO BE PHYSICALLY
NEAR SOMEONE TO HEAL THEM.
Distance IS NOT A FACTOR.

Adam

CHAPTER 6

Healing Histories

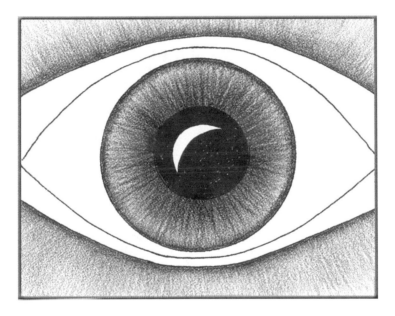

I HAVE ENJOYED WORKING WITH MANY PEOPLE AND FIND HEALING COMES naturally FOR ME.

Adam

HEALING HISTORIES

"Miracles do not happen
in contradiction to nature,
but only in contradiction to
that which is known to us in nature."

-St. Augustine

The energy work that I do is a manipulation of internal energy, which in turn is reflected, in the external aura of a person. This is a deep and permanent healing.

I go into the person's quantum hologram to view the inside of the body. At this point I use my energy, theirs and the surrounding energy to focus on removing energy blockages which are causing the disease or highlighting the injured area. An injury or diseased area stands out as a bright green. Past injuries are seen as a darker green. When I am viewing inside people, I also have intuitive knowledge of what and where the problem is. This is very difficult to explain in words. Basically, I travel through the person's body and observe. This process I refer to as seeing.

When I first started to heal, I was only looking at the most basic energy level. Now I am able to view many levels at a time. I view several holograms of the person for energy diagnosis and healing. I am also able to bring up another person's hologram along side to compare the different functions of the body. This is a handy tool for me when I am not sure what a normal functioning body should look like. Now my healings are much more effective because I can approach the illness or injury from several different fronts. I know there are many more levels for me to develop as I get more experienced.

Another important development of my gift is the ability to go down to the cellular level and actually **see** whether cells have a pre-cancerous or abnormal state which may lead to trouble in the future. This is extremely important in energetically diagnosing illnesses prior to a dangerous situation developing.

I have enjoyed working with many people and find healing comes naturally for me. At first, it was important for me to work within a confidential and isolated group in order to develop and understand my gift. My school life and personal friends had to be kept separate from my healing work. For this reason I saw people whom my parents knew weren't associated with friends my own age. Most came as nonbelievers and skeptics, and left in awe.

As my skills developed and people started hearing about me by word-of-mouth, I started to be contacted by others in the healing profession. I worked with a group of naturopathic doctors who consulted me when the patient was interested in my ability. One patient was an elderly lady with an extremely sore leg. I immediately pointed to an area on her hip as the source, which was nowhere near the pain. The area I pointed to is where two muscle groups meet and when the doctor touched the area on her hip, the lady's leg flew up and nearly kicked him.

"That's it!" she exclaimed. "That's where the problem is!"

It was a great experience for me to see this process in action. I was given no background information about the patients before hand, yet every diagnosis I gave was accurate.

My Most Difficult Healing

Last year my parents decided to take the family to Mexico for a break from all the healing and e-mails. I felt that I needed a 'brain break' and I knew that a break would make me more powerful. We also thought that it would be exciting to spend Christmas in a different country.

The vacation was off to a great start. The resort where we stayed was part of an 'all inclusive' package, so my sister and I could order drinks all day. My Dad made sure the bartender knew how old we were. As soon as we arrived, he took my sister and me to meet the bartender. He introduced us as his son and daughter and informed him that "they don't drink alcohol." We were able to order endless virgin strawberry daiquiris though.

Two days into our vacation my Dad was playing with my sister and I in the resort pool. Dad had just thrown my sister up into the air and over his head. At the same time, I was just swimming out of the water behind him.

The timing couldn't have been worse.

My sister landed on my head causing a fracture in one of my neck vertebrae. I felt numbness spreading down my body. It was a cold feeling. I somehow managed to get out of the water before I lost feeling in my legs.

My parents immediately called an ambulance. The pain in my neck was unlike anything I had ever experienced. I felt like I should pass out, but I knew I was the only one who could fix my neck. I knew it was bad, because I could go in and see it.

It was very difficult to heal myself because I was in excruciating pain. When I try to view an injury in my own body it always looks foggy to me. I had to try my hardest and use all the power at my disposal. I worked on the fracture and the swelling for about half an hour. In that time I could see that I had managed to heal the fracture and bring the swelling down. It is important to reduce the swelling as quickly as possible, because the swelling itself can create further problems. By the time the ambulance arrived, I was actually walking, but the attendants insisted I put on a neck brace and go to the hospital.

When I arrived at the hospital they immediately started taking x-rays. The neurologist arrived with his little reflex hammer. He checked to see that all my reflexes were working, and I passed with flying colors. When they looked at the x-rays, the doctors pointed out that I had a congenital defect on my C2 vertebra. Otherwise, everything was fine.

I knew that it was not a congenital defect. It was the area that I had just damaged and subsequently healed. My parents brought the x-rays home with us so that we could compare them with ones taken a few years ago when I injured my shoulder playing tennis. As I expected, there was no sign of a congenital defect on the earlier x-rays.

I felt that I had just passed a major test of willpower and healing ability. I surprised even myself with what one can do if confronted with the need. It was more difficult than any other healing I had done.

Chronic Illness

Living with chronic illness is a reality for millions of people. It affects adults as well as children. Out of necessity, people get used to tolerating constant pain, so this becomes the normal state of health. Many have forgotten the pain-free time of their lives. In order to heal they must first remember this. They must have a contrast in their mind and set their goal accordingly.

A number of people have come to me with chronic illness. Because it has been with them for so many years (hence, categorized as chronic) many think that it might take a lot of work to fix. Sometimes it does, but not always.

Under the traditional medical system there are no cures for many illnesses, just ways to manage and live with them. Sadly, this has caused some people to give up hope of ever getting better. However, I have treated a number of these people and their pain is sometimes eliminated within two or three treatments. Often one treatment produces amazing results. These results have been long lasting and in many cases the chronic problem has been eliminated.

One individual came to me with a sore neck that had bothered him for four years. I had no problem finding the problem and I spent about five minutes treating him. He reported that he felt immediate relief. He was amazed that for the first time in four years his neck was not sore or stiff. I guess he felt so good that he decided to go skiing. Unfortunately, he re-injured his neck and I had to do another treatment. The second treatment was also successful but this time I made sure that he understood that muscles and ligaments take a bit of time to adjust to the new state of wellness. As such, I asked him to refrain from any physical strain (such as skiing) for a while.

The return to health is a *process*. Because it is a process, a sequence of changes must occur. The mind is already there or the healing wouldn't have occurred. The mind and the body are connected, but the mind can get there quicker than the physical body. People I have treated must gradually let their body catch up. It takes time. Those who have suffered with chronic pain for years frequently over exert themselves at first. They feel so good, and are so glad to be pain free. In their enthusiasm, they sometimes return to activities which they have been unable to do for a long time, but BEFORE the body has had a chance to finish the healing process. It is very important to give the body sufficient time to complete the process.

Another fellow came to me with a sore back that had bothered him for years. When I went in I could see that the third and fifth disks in his lower back were damaged. He confirmed that these areas had been diagnosed as the problem, but didn't know there was anything that could be done about it. I treated him, and his back pain has improved considerably. He returns from time to time for maintenance treatments. It is very rewarding for me to be able to help people who have suffered for years.

I had the pleasure of meeting a woman, who was planning her wedding, yet was in too much pain to try on shoes for her big day. After treating her I received the following testimonial:

"I was diagnosed with fibromyalgia when I was 12 years old. My whole life changed at the first onset of the symptoms. I was physically unable to do the fun things a

12-year-old girl should have no problems with. I had been in figure skating competitions, was an avid skier and very much into horse back riding and mountain biking. I was depressed when these activities proved to be too much for my body to handle. I cried often with the pains in my legs and arms and my sleepless nights grew more frequent. I was lucky to have a few years of remission in my late teens, but after a car accident I was again disabled with fibromyalgia and unable to work for years.

When I was 25, I returned to work for a few years coping with the pain as best I could, sometimes better than others. Then I was introduced to Adam. I was told he had special abilities to heal people. How? By looking inside them. With nothing to lose I went to visit him one Wednesday after work.

He looked and said he would be able to help me with three treatments and with my permission he began treatment. I felt tingles all through my body and tried to be calm and relaxed while Adam seemed to stare at something no one else in the room could see. It is hard to explain how it felt. At times it was just goose bumps on my arms and legs and at other times I felt as if a tornado was moving inside my chest. It was never painful but more mysterious than anything.

According to the people in the room I went quite pale. I felt faint and shaky after the treatment and I was very quiet for several hours afterward. I feel in part, that this was because I was contemplating what had just happened inside my body but partly because I did not feel myself. I felt as if my skin were crawling. In the past I had taken muscle relaxants and when they began to wear off I would feel this same sensation in my skin. It was not painful but annoying.

I slept through the night until the alarm went off the next morning. I did not wake up once to roll over as I usually did several times throughout the night. When I woke up I felt refreshed and full of energy. I continued to feel like this for the next few days.

My next treatment with Adam was done long distance on a Sunday morning. I sat in a comfortable chair with a blanket around me, both feet on the floor. I felt the same feelings of goose bumps and tornadoes. I fell asleep and felt fine afterwards. Days later I had my third treatment with Adam and experienced the very same sensations.

On my fourth and final visit I experienced the same feelings during my treatment but afterwards was feeling not quite myself. I was very tired and my skin was hyper-

sensitive. I was so exhausted I fell asleep around 9 p.m. (early for me) and slept through my alarm the next morning.

That day I felt energized and full of life. I have big dreams of beginning to work out again but I will take it one day at a time.

I feel better. I sleep better and I have an easier time coping with the day-to-day activities that used to drain me. Although I do experience little flashes or glimpses of the pains that I used to have, it is nothing compared to experiencing them all the time.

Adam has a kind and gentle soul. This is apparent the first time you meet him. He will do great things and I am blessed to have been helped by him."

Another fellow from Chicago I treated for chronic conditions had been involved in a bad car accident many years ago. He had very little success from conventional medicine, yet after several treatments, he sent me the following message:

"I am amazed by the first treatment when I experienced significant improvement in focus and concentration. In my opinion, you are one of the most precise healers com-

pared to all the other healers I have met throughout the world. Everything looks great and the changes feel like they are permanent. I have experienced the following improvements:

- Overall I feel much better (calmed down).

- No headaches since we started treatments.

- No more stomach aches.

- Digestive system works much better."

A lady in her forties from Hawaii had severe chronic asthma for many years. This was her response after one treatment:

"Thank you very much for using your gift to help me. My breathing was much heavier before the treatment. My mind seems clearer. I have noticed a definite improvement and this is only one session. While I sat on my couch at 4:30 p.m. I felt heat on my throat and chest area and a tingling feeling throughout my arms and legs. My breathing was faster and heavier. During the healing, I could feel my breathing slow down. I was so relaxed that I fell asleep. I woke up at 4:33 a.m. I still feel healing or warm pressure on my throat and chest."

Another lady in her 50's with peripheral neuropathy (painful nerve sensation) wrote:

"I want to thank you so much for what you have done for me. I no longer experience the discomfort that peripheral neuropathy has caused me. The feelings of numbness, 'pins and needles,' and 'burning sensation' in my hands and feet no longer exist. You have been able to give me back my quality of life that was quickly fading away."

In another situation, a lady who called me had chronic stomach problems and indicated to me that she ate poorly and felt tired most of the time. In addition, she said she slept poorly and suffered from occasional moments of depression. This is what she wrote after the first treatment:

"I woke up this morning and my stomach was not in pain as it always is. I didn't have trouble taking deep breaths and although the pain on my liver was not as constant as my stomach discomfort, I feel none right now. I will keep you posted. Although I express primarily through music and words, neither are enough right now to thank you for working on this with me. I felt desperate and you have given me back my peace. This is honestly the first time I've heard about this type of treatment, but I firmly believe. I can't thank you enough."

Here's a testimonial from a quadriplegic after one treatment. I should mention that I had cautioned him to

95

have no expectations going into this since his spine had been completely severed.

"I really noticed some things tonight. There is a tingling sensation in my triceps muscles, the muscles at the back of my upper arms. These muscles have not moved or had feeling in 20 years. It's quite exciting. Also I have chronic soreness and stiffness in my neck and shoulder joints. This is greatly reduced tonight. And my entire lower body has a gentle, almost imperceptible tingling."

One year while on vacation with my family we met a lady, who had been diagnosed with syringomyelia, which is a degenerative spinal condition. She was told that she was one of a very small group of people who have this particular form of the disease. This was her response after a few treatments:

"My year has started off unbelievably!!! I feel absolutely wonderful. Not all my pain is gone, but I would say that at least 75 percent has gone. I don't know how to thank you. I can stand up properly now and can roll over in bed, which I haven't been able to do without pain for a long, long, time. Thank you!"

CANCER

One of the things that I found immediately interesting was how it looked when I saw someone who was undergoing, or had undergone, chemotherapy. Inside their body it looks like a war zone. Cells are fighting each other in an exhaustive battle of survival, and it doesn't look like there are any real victors.

When I go in to a person with cancer or a tumor, I am often amazed by how fast these things can grow. If the cancer is advanced through the person's entire system, it is almost impossible to stay ahead of the growth. I am much more optimistic about my ability to help when it has not spread. If it is in an isolated area (such as an organ) I am quite confident that I can do something with it.

Standard therapies to destroy tumor cells range from radiation to chemical treatments, often causing side effects. Radiation is energy that is used to alter the genetic code of a cell. It is a hit-and-miss procedure. The genetic code tells the cell how to grow and divide, thus spreading the cancer. Radiation also attacks normal cells, which in turn causes side effects. It is a delicate balance between eliminating cancer cells and sparing normal cells. In a lot of situations with radiation, the individual's life can be prolonged. During this extended life span, chemotherapy is usually necessary, which adds more side effects to a body that is already ravaged. Of course in some situations chemotherapy and radiation is very successful. In making these decisions, the quality of life should be an issue.

I am able to go in and alter the genetic code of the cancer cells on the energetic level. Another important property of cancer cells is that they communicate with one another. When they communicate, they pass on this genetic change to other cancer cells and the death of the cancer spreads in a chain reaction. None of the healthy cells are damaged because they were not modified. The only small side effects are from the body adjusting to being healthy again.

This technique is only applicable to cancer that is localized like a single tumor, rather than a malignant spread. Imagine a 'sealed in' city occupied by cancer cells with no communication to the outside world. The only communication is with one another. When I make changes they spread the good news around to each other, causing their destruction.

If the cancer is spread out, as it is with some cancers like advanced lung cancers, there are cancer cells outside the 'city' that could warn the rest of the cancer and prevent the changes required to kill them off. In this situation, I would resort to a combination of reasonably high intensity of yellow, purple and white light energy. I would not use light that is focussed like a laser because the cancer is spread out too much for that to be effective.

Sometimes during treatment, the person can feel the activity or process. Some people describe it as a tingling sensation in the area that I am treating. Others experience it as like having a whole bunch of tiny little ping-pong balls ricocheting inside them. On occasion, some people feel really sleepy or even dizzy or nauseous. And some people feel nothing. Everyone is different. How they feel it, or even if they feel it, doesn't seem to matter to the outcome of my treatment. Some people have immediately fallen fast asleep so it is important that at the exact time of treatment they are seated comfortably.

The Healer & The Hawk

Healing Ronnie Hawkins

On September 21, 2002 I noticed an article in our local paper on the rock legend Ronnie Hawkins. It was reported that he had been diagnosed with inoperable pancreatic cancer. I had never heard of Ronnie Hawkins before that day, but my Dad said he enjoys his music.

Ronnie Hawkins has lived in Canada in the Toronto, Ontario area since the late 1950s when he immigrated to Canada from his native Arkansas. Many consider Ronnie to have been the performer who brought rock and roll to Canada back then. Ronnie is perhaps best known outside of Canada for some of the major stars whom at one time or another played in his backing band. For example, the original name for "The Band," legendary in the 1960s and early 1970s for backing Bob Dylan, was "The Hawks," Ronnie's backing band. Of course, the Band were also huge stars in their own right. Ronnie has known everyone in the business for decades. When John Lennon and Yoko Ono were in town during their peace crusade in late 1969, they stayed at Ronnie's place.

I had not healed anyone of pancreatic cancer before but I wanted to try and help. On August 13, 2002, Ronnie had gone into surgery so the doctors could try to remove the tumor. However, when they cut him open they realized that the tumor was much larger than the 3 cm they had anticipated. It was wrapped around an artery so they couldn't remove it. It said in the article that chemotherapy was not an option. He was terminal, so I thought he might be interested in my healing ability.

I contacted Ronnie's daughter-in-law Mary, who is his manager. She was very open-minded and felt that they had nothing to lose. From talking to Mary, I realized that Ronnie wasn't just a rock legend but a loving husband, father of three and grandfather. There were a lot of concerned and worried relatives.

Another unusual aspect of my gift is intuitiveness. When I looked at Ronnie's photo, my first impression was that he was an honest man. When I told Mary this she said that comment shook her. She said that Ronnie is as honest as they come, and he is one of the funniest people you will ever meet. Ronnie was quite willing to try my healing approach, since the doctors had basically written him off. Distant healing was certainly a new idea to Ronnie and his family, but they were keen to give it a try.

"If Adam can pull this off, tell him we'll send him an autographed Hawk T-shirt." Ronnie said with his trademark good humor. "Five of the best doctors in the world have told me that this is it. They said 3-6 months, tops — I'm gone."

This information about Ronnie's dire state of health triggered a landslide of concern for Ronnie from within the music industry. He had touched so many people over the span of his career.

In September, well-known Canadian producer/composer David Foster, also an alumnus of Ronnie's backing band, hosted an intimate private gathering in Ronnie's honor in Toronto with major celebrities attending. Included were former President Bill Clinton, comedienne Whoopi Goldberg, singer/composer Paul Anka, Ronnie's tycoon friend Don Tyson from Arkansas and Canadian industrialist Peter Pocklington. Paul Anka even rewrote a version of his song "*My Way*" and dedicated it to Ronnie. Bill Clinton, David Foster and Paul Anka sang their parts to this song, which was the highlight of the evening. Ronnie, with his wife Wanda at his side, had his guests laughing through their tears the entire time.

A few weeks later, the City of Toronto declared October 4th as Ronnie Hawkins Day. The 4th started off with Ronnie being inducted into Canada's Walk of Fame. Many people feel that it was an induction that was long overdue. Normally, this recognition is made in May of each year. However, because of the expected urgency with Ronnie's health, it was done in October 2002. That evening, a tribute concert was held at Massey Hall to honor Ronnie. Even Ronnie himself got up on stage and joined his band with the song "Hey Bo Diddley." Kris Kristofferson and the Tragically Hip highlighted a very special four-hour concert of stars.

"If there is a God of rock and roll, I know he looks just like this guy," Kris Kristofferson said in his tribute.

Ronnie got lots of press in October 2002 because of the concerns about his health. Someone said Ronnie was on the front page of newspapers at least 17 times within that one-month period.

When I first went into Ronnie's hologram on September 21, 2002, I could see a tumor about the size of a tennis ball (approximately 10-cm). I spent the next few weeks treating Ronnie's tumor on the energetic level, helping Ronnie's body fight off the cancer and reduce the tumor. From the beginning of my treatment Ronnie felt a quivering in his stomach area. His jaundice improved and his overall observed health was getting better. He no longer felt or looked like a dying man. The first time we heard that he looked wonderful was September 23, 2002, so everyone was very encouraged, especially Ronnie. He told me to "KEEP ON ROCKIN'."

I continued treating Ronnie every day very intensely because we were all so positive about it. On September 27, 2002, I energetically compared Ronnie's pancreatic functioning to my Dad's. I did this by visually bringing in front of me the quantum hologram screens of both. I noticed that Ronnie's pancreas was blocked and my Dad's had a constant drip flowing out of it. I manipulated the energy and got Ronnie's pancreatic juices flowing. It actually started with a gushing flow from what I saw energetically, as there was probably a lot of build-up. My parents spent a sleepless night worrying about this, but I assured them that his body knows how to regulate it. I later found out that the pancreas secretes insulin and many enzymes which would have been blocked by the tumor.

Ronnie continued to feel and look great, and his blood sugar levels improved. He was walking better and his eyes looked clearer. Ronnie *wanted* to get better. He has such a love for life. This is his greatest strength.

By the time November arrived, rather than planning a funeral, he was planning a CD release and a new TV show. Ronnie continued to feel better and the fluttering feeling in his abdomen persisted. I could see energetically that the cancer was gone, and that the remaining tumor tissue, no longer growing, was being removed by Ronnie's own system. This takes time, so the quivering feeling continued.

A CT scan was done on November 14, 2002 and it determined that the tumor was approximately 4.5 cm. Considering the original 10 cm mass I saw on the energetic level, the tumor had shrunk in half. But the doctors still believed that Ronnie had cancer and he was going to die.

Ronnie went in for a biopsy on November 27, 2002 to check on the cancer. The doctors said that they got a good sized tissue sample so they should be able to find the cancer, if it was there. However, the biopsy turned out to be negative. In other words, there was *no cancer*.

All the treatments I did were from 3000 miles away. I started working on Ronnie's energy system September 21, 2002, a month and a half after the surgeon sewed him back up indicating there wasn't anything else they could do for him. The doctors expected that he would not live to see Christmas 2002. I treated his energy system on a daily basis for a few weeks and fairly regularly after that. All my indications on the energy level were that his body had managed to kill the cancer and the tumor was shrinking very rapidly.

"Ronnie feels great!" is what I hear from those who are close to him. I have yet to meet him in person, but I hope that one day we have the opportunity.

In January 2003 I was pleased to hear that Ronnie quit smoking. He is very strong willed and I know he will stay with it. Ronnie said that he feels like he could beat his son Robin running up and down the stairs and wants to join his former hockey team. He has been successful at losing weight to increase his fitness level and is now thinking more about living than dying. This psychological shift will no doubt see him to his dream of wellness.

On February 27th Ronnie went for a CT scan which showed no evidence of any tumor remaining. He now performs on stage with his band and sings all night. This is an amazing change because it was only months before that he was a dying man. An MRI was done April 11, 2003 and it confirms Ronnie is cancer-free.

And I expect my Hawk T-shirt should arrive in the mail any day now!

Here is Ronnie Hawkins' testimonial. It is sincere and heartfelt, and I feel very privileged to have this opportunity to share it with you.

"After the diagnosis, I put myself in The Big Rocker's hands and now I know it wasn't my time . . . as Adam kept telling me over and over. Well, I've come to believe that The Big Rocker works in mysterious ways and He was listening to all those wonderful folks who sent out prayers for me. Adam got in touch with me and helped me to believe in myself again. Pretty soon after his treatments started, he told me the cancer was gone. For whatever it is that Adam does, whatever he did for me, I don't understand it and I don't criticize what I don't understand. I know Adam can't help everyone on the planet, but I hope people will believe that there is more to our world than we can

see and understand. It is important that we believe in ourselves and know that the Big Rocker is always watching out for us. I know I'm glad that He put Adam on my case and I'm so very thankful to Adam for everything."

Ronnie Hawkins, April 9, 2003

Press Release April 23, 2003

HAWK IS CLEARED FOR TAKEOFF!

Doctors have confirmed that the latest tests on Ronnie Hawkins have showed there is no evidence of cancer. Canada's legendary rocker was diagnosed with cancer of the pancreas in the summer of 2002. A CT scan and an MRI in April of 2003 showed that Ronnie is free of disease. No further problems from this condition are expected.

"I couldn't be happier," said the Hawk, getting off the phone from one of his doctors who called with the good news. "Few months back I thought all those girls had nothin' to worry about. Turns out they better start runnin'! Now, I'm back and ready to rock!"

Ronnie and his family wish to thank all of the fans all over the world for their prayers and support during this very difficult time. Musicians gathered at many locations to pay tribute to Ronnie in the past 12 months including major shows at Massey Hall and in Hamilton. Ronnie Hawkins is acknowledged as one of the leading influences in Rock 'n Roll, credited with helping hundreds of international musicians, including The Band, achieve remarkable success.

Ronnie is very thankful that a 16-year-old healer named Adam got in touch with him and they worked together treating his cancer until it was gone. A book called "DreamHealer" explains the type of treatment that was successfully done on Ronnie over the past 7 months. (See Ronnie Hawkins website - www.ronniehawkins.com)

— 30 —

Ronnie's office confirmed that The Hawk is working hard this spring and ready for a busy schedule of shows this summer.

"The Big Rocker helped me and I want to get back out there to thank Him!" Ronnie said in an interview today. (April 23, 2003)

I HOPE PEOPLE WILL believe THAT THERE IS MORE TO OUR WORLD THAN WE CAN SEE AND UNDERSTAND.

Ronnie Hawkins

CHAPTER 7

The Learning
Continues

WHAT IS IN THE mind IS ALWAYS REFLECTED IN THE body.

Adam

The Learning Continues

What have I learned from healing people? I have learned many things. For one thing, I learned that disease starts in a person's energy field and shows as a blockage of the energy flow in the body. And as I've said before, often this can be visible to someone like me before the person feels any of the symptoms. Disease as a word can be separated into DIS- meaning opposite, and EASE as the flow of healthy, harmonious energy. DIS-EASE is the unpatterned result of an energy blockage.

Most diseases or illnesses have their own 'signature' or similar appearance in the hologram which I view. This revelation became clear to me after treating many people with similar problems. Each person is an individual and his or her journey to wellness is an individual process. Healing a *person* rather than just eliminating the ailment is vital. People react differently to every type of treatment, whether using conventional medicine or energy healing.

Sometimes the cause of disease is a poor lifestyle choice such as improper diet, lack of exercise, smoking, drinking or excessive drugs (either street drugs or prescription drugs). I've had to set some pretty tough boundaries if they continue making choices contrary to their health. For example, when a person with a smoking-related disease continues to smoke, treating them would not result in a cure, as the root cause of the problem has not been addressed.

I could see abnormal cells developing in a man I treated. I knew that if this person continued to smoke cigarettes there would be no point in giving him healing energy as the cancer would regenerate faster than I could kill it. I informed him that he *had* to quit smoking, and he did when I told him that I would not attempt further treatments until he did. Often lifestyle changes *must* be made in order for the person to be healed.

It is also very difficult for me to see clearly inside bodies of people who are on medications. Sometimes I am able to time my treatment to just before it is time for a person to take their medication. This usually allows me to see clearly enough to carry out a treatment. Of course, any change in your medication must be done through your Physician.

I saw a 40-year-old woman who had been in a debilitating car accident and as a result was on painkillers and anti-inflammatory drugs. I found that the medications made the energy blockages like jelly to work with during treatments, thus I was unable to move them. I suggested that she reschedule another treatment time that was just *before* she took her medication. When she did, I found her energy blockages much easier to move, and she reported that she noticed the positive effects more intensely.

Muscular and structural maladies are fairly straight-forward. They are easy for me to spot on the body as I see breaks in the person's aura. I can go in and show the body its natural energy grid. Sometimes the injury or whatever is causing the malady is so old that the body has forgotten what the natural healthy state is like. It is very helpful if I can show the map of health, as the body is an amazing thing and will strive to return to a healthy state if given the chance. The body would then know and remember what its healthy state should be. Showing the body this ideal state and providing a push in the right direction is sometimes all that is needed.

Another thing I learned is that some people have underlying psychological and/or emotional issues, which affect the energy body and must be addressed BEFORE a person can be healed. A person's own negativity, guilt, or fear will work against their path to wellness. Be prepared for some personal work and perhaps some lifestyle changes if you want to achieve a lasting state of wellness.

I remember one lady I went in to help and thought that I couldn't do anything for her. The medications she had taken prevented me from doing my healing. She said she had just taken her antidepressants prior to the treatment, so we rescheduled another healing before she took her medication. This time I was able to remove some energy blockages, but I intuitively noted a strong psychological basis to the illness. She mentioned that before I treated her, there were about five other unrelated problems that were bothering her. It was evident to me that the scattering of complaints was largely emotionally based negativity. My feeling was that she needed to address this before I could improve her state of wellness. I presently need more experience in order to help with psychological problems.

Occasionally the treated person does not accept the new pattern of health. If the illness or injury serves another purpose, the person may hold on to the 'dis-ease.' For example, I treated one gentleman who complained of a stomach condition that was similar in symptoms to those experienced by people with IBS (irritable bowel syndrome). Those symptoms include abdominal pains, severe diarrhea and reactions to certain foods. He claimed to be allergic to milk or dairy products and took great pains to avoid them.

I went in and took a look. I could see that his stomach was irritated, but I could see no physical reason or cause. I am not saying that it was all in his head. I know that the symptoms he experienced were very real to him (and painful). It seemed to me that he processed his emotions and his anxieties through his stomach. I suspect that if he didn't create the stomach condition, he may have had to create another physical malady.

I could treat this gentleman every day, but his condition would always return unless he formed a new strategy to deal with and/or process his emotions. The body is amazingly complicated in that our health involves a mind/body connection. What is in the mind is always reflected in the body.

I have also learned that some people have difficulty accepting their newfound wellness. Illness serves another purpose that they believe is very important to them. If they become well, the purpose served by the illness is not achieved.

Sometimes the real reason a person becomes ill is because they have been seriously disappointed and have become disenchanted with life. This is a form of retaliation. They may feel that life has injured them, and they retaliate by not fully participating.

There are many psychological reasons for illness. What is in the mind directly affects the body. When someone feels deprived of attention and recognition, illness (particularly if it is chronic) can cause the person to receive that wanted attention and recognition. This can range from needing a special diet to being completely bedridden. The disease becomes reality in the body because of what was first perceived by the mind. For the body to return to a state of total health, the issues of attention and recognition must be addressed. You can't just heal the body and expect lasting effects if the mind is not in alignment with this objective.

Another root cause of disease is related to avoidance behavior. A person, for instance, may be suffering with a work-related injury because what the mind has created is a desire for a new career. But that can be a scary thing, even if the person wants it. A drastic life change is not an easy thing for many people to make. Creating the chronic condition replaces the desired change. It all depends on what is most important to the person.

Other family members can also be a factor in our health situation. One time a lady emailed me in a panic with terminal cancer. She did not want to pursue chemotherapy or radiation so she wanted to explore energy healing. As I said before, it is never just one person in the family affected by the illness. Her family wanted her to have chemotherapy and radiation. Even after x-rays showed that the tumors had significantly shrunk after my treatments, she continued to waffle about chemotherapy because of the pressures from relatives. Eventually she decided to go with chemotherapy.

For the most part, however, people are ready, willing and accepting of my energy treatments. With that receptivity and a positive attitude, I have had the honor and pleasure of helping many people return to health.

For some people however, it just appears to be their time. A man from out of town whose father was in an extended care hospital after suffering a stroke contacted me. The son was concerned that his father was dying. I went to the hospital where his father was so that I could do an 'in person' treatment on him. He was lying in bed and was non-responsive when I first saw him. During the treatment, I saw a strong spirit in the man, and I could tell that it was not his time to go yet, but that it was near. The next day after only one treatment, he was able to sit up, talk and even complain about the food. A couple of months later his entire family came from out of the country to visit him. By this time, he was even well enough to go with all of them to his favorite restaurant, and he even purchased a lottery ticket. He died later during their visit, but he died peacefully, knowing that it was his time and that he had been able to say his good-byes to those he loved.

Another thing I have learned is that most people are only interested in my type of healing as a LAST resort, rather than a first choice. This doesn't make sense to me, as I personally would be most interested in trying the least invasive treatment first.

I was contacted several times by people who have cancer and as a result they have been through operations, chemotherapy, and radiation. Now that they are terminal, they ask for my help. Every cell in their body is either cancerous or extremely affected by the disease and/or the medical treatments, which they have undergone. I cannot take on such cases, as the energy required for this would threaten my own health. I always wish they could have contacted me earlier. But, as I said, energy healing is often considered only as a last resort, after every other avenue has been exhausted. By the time they come to me, they are in pretty bad shape and with nowhere to turn. I hope my abilities will change enough in the future so I can help these people as well.

I had a father e-mail me a week before Christmas with an urgent plea. His son had leukemia with a fever of 105 degrees Fahrenheit and blood in his urine. He and his wife were living in a motel near the hospital where his son had been a patient for many months. He had no idea how he was going to pay for the $100,000 hospital bill that was climbing each day. All he and his wife knew is they desperately wanted their son to get better.

When I looked at the boy, I knew right away that his body had already decided to shut down. All I could do was give him positive encouragement and some energy. I managed to get his temperature down below a hundred degrees for a couple of days. He was actually able to get out of bed and play with a few of his toys. This was something he had not done for weeks. However the illness was too far along to halt and he passed away on Christmas Eve. It was very sad. I wish he had contacted me sooner.

You never realize how many sick people there are in the world until you are able to do something about it. The problem is, I am not able to help everyone. So I have to make some tough decisions when it comes to deciding who to treat. Telling a person that there is nothing I can do is very difficult. However, it is something that has to be done. I only hope I can give bits of advice that might make their lives a little more comfortable.

Most of the people I see are usually in need of some positive thoughts as part of their healing. By the time they have turned to something 'radical' like energy healing, they most often have already been turned away by the traditional medical system. Being told that there is nothing more that can be done and that you will probably die in six months is not easy to hear. I understand that doctors have to make these types of decisions every day. I also understand that there is a point in an illness when we have to face the music.

Sometimes being told that you will probably die in six months may be self-fulfilling. Keep in mind, the brain is like a super computer controlled by thought messages. In addition to our own thoughts, it is constantly being fed information by those around us and will respond to positive or negative thoughts accordingly. We must take control of this computer rather than allowing it to control us. What I am suggesting is that no one should rush quickly to conclusions when there might be something that can be done. Exhaust *all* possibilities.

The human body is much more than an extremely complicated machine. Everything is interconnected and one change or dysfunction affects everything else. This is very important for people to realize. Within this interconnectedness, everything has a purpose.

Unity

A vast similitude interlocks all,
All spheres, grown, ungrown, small.
large, suns, moon, planets,
All distances of place however wide,
All distances of time, all inanimate forms,
All souls, all living bodies though they be ever so
different, or in different worlds,
All gaseous, watery, vegetable, mineral processes,
the fishes, the brutes,
All nations, colors, barbarisms, civilizations, languages,
All identities that have existed or may exist
on this globe, or any globe,
All lives, and deaths, all of the past, present, future,
This vast similitude spans them,
and always has spann'd,
And shall forever span them and compactly hold
and enclose them.

- From Leaves of Grass, by Walt Whitman

YOU MUST STEP OUT OF THE BOX OF CONVENTIONAL THINKING. YOU NEED courage TO TAKE THAT STEP.

Adam

CHAPTER 8

The Return to Health

Is a Process

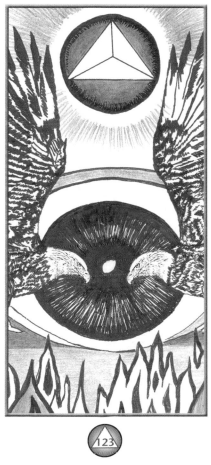

FROM BEGINNING TO END,
Attitude IS IMPORTANT.
Rachel Orr

The Return to Health is a Process

Stated as simply as possible, disease is the absence of health. It is an energy system out of balance. It is a body that is not recognizing its natural grid, or code for proper function.

Disease can take many forms. Sometimes it shows itself as chronic pain. Sometimes the body will grow a tumor. Sometimes it will grow cancer. There are many ways that disease can manifest itself, and there are just as many causes for it.

Ideal health would be a state of no energy blockages where energy flows freely throughout the body both internally and through the external reflection of this. Everything works together in perfect harmony. There would be no physical, energetic, or emotional conflict in the body. Perfect balance would exist.

It would be incredibly difficult to achieve perfect health, yet it should be everyone's goal. Old scars and injuries make this impossible, but we can, and should, work toward achieving the best balance possible within these limitations.

Attitude

From beginning to end, attitude is important. I don't think that my spiritual belief system has any impact on my healing work. Whatever a person's religious or spiritual guidance is, it should be maintained as it is important to them and therefore to the healing process. Most important is a positive attitude. *Believe* that good things are going to happen.

Attitude is a very powerful tool in the healing process and is the foundation for returning ones body to good health. A person must be able to show thanks to others and be thankful for the good things in their life. By dwelling on the bad things in our lives, we are unable to appreciate all the good.

You must step out of the box of conventional think-ing. You need courage to take that step. There is no author-ity other than you as to whether healing (or anything else, for that matter) is going to work. People delegate authority to others who are deemed as experts. Perhaps they feel that it relieves them of the responsibility, but it doesn't. The choice and authority is still ultimately yours. Courage and positive attitude will lead you along your path to wellness.

Having an open mind helps you achieve any goal. I believe that everyone has a certain degree of power to heal themselves and others. It is just that some people are more sensitive to the universal energy connection.

Similarly, some of us are much better than others at playing the piano, or playing sports. The point is that we may not all be Mozart's or Tiger Woods, but we can all learn to play the piano or golf if we dedicate the time and focus. I think it's the same for what I do. We can all do it, it is just that some of us are more naturally gifted, or better at it than others. As I've said, we all have our gifts. They are all equally precious. Each of us can achieve our own personal best with a positive attitude.

Worry is a Waste

Worry is a total waste of time. It is fear of the future, which has yet to be determined. It is harmful. It is harmful to the worrier and everyone else. Nothing good comes of worry.

Worry leads to guilt. Guilt leads to negativity and loss of self-empowerment, and then it effects our health. And then it affects everyone around you through our interconnectedness. Some people are so disconnected from themselves and their own energy system, that relating to others and the connectedness is very challenging.

Worry can bring on and cause dis-ease. I can make the body aware that things can be different, but unless the person can see through their own negativity, nothing will change. This will affect the efficacy of the treatments. It is far easier to treat someone with terminal cancer and a positive attitude than someone who has a minor ailment in comparison, but a negative attitude.

Some people cannot get out of their negative thought-loop. If you say to them "Hey, isn't it a wonderful sunny day?" they reply with something like "Yeah, but it's probably going to rain tomorrow." They are insulated by negativity. From past experiences, they paste various negative labels on life. The excuses range from parents to guilt issues. They tend to blame others, especially their parents, but that is useless. Whatever your excuse is, you've got to get over it.

Visualizing & Intuitiveness

"Imagination is more important than knowledge, because imagination encircles the world."
- Albert Einstein

NEVER underestimate the power of self-visualization. When you are imagining, you are visualizing. When you are visualizing, you are accessing the universal knowledge base, more scientifically known as the field of quantum information. Intuition is the ability to tap into this field that surrounds all of us and emanates throughout the universe.

See yourself in the state of wellness you want to achieve. Do this in as much detail as you can. This is your personal goal, your dream. *See* yourself doing what you will do in this state of wellness. *Feel* how it will feel in this state. *Hear* the sounds you will hear around you. *Smell* the air. Do this everyday. Make time for it, and look forward to spending this time with yourself each day.

Therapists have helped people by suggestion. They ask their patients to visualize the illness in their body and then have them visualize its removal by various means. When doing this, the mind is basically telling the body to heal itself. This might be very successful with a few people who have a very vivid imagination and are able to hold the healing thoughts for long periods of time.

What I do is similar except that I influence the mind/body controls and bypass the person's need to successfully carry out the task of visualization. If someone were able to do this suggestive visualization while I do my healing, then that would make my job easier. Your dream of your path to wellness will help you achieve your goal.

My ability to tap into the knowledge base that surrounds us is always increasing. When I first started healing I would have to see a picture of someone in order to receive any information on them. Now, when someone just mentions a name, I automatically make the connection to that person. When I tap into information on a person this way, it goes through the person mentioning the name, so if someone else has the same name I still connect to the right person. The path of linking to another person happens too fast to understand or map out.

Intuitiveness works in many strange ways. My parents were going to a friend's house for dinner one night and they told me who was going to be there. The name of one person brought an image into my mind about his ex-wife. He had been separated for 10 years. I mentioned that she had some kind of neurological problem that was affecting her reasoning. I also said that this happened about 10 years ago and she is doing much better now. At dinner my parents confirmed that all of this had taken place.

I usually know or sense what is wrong with a person before they say anything or before I go in and see. I get way more detail when I actually go in and look at the person's energy system. This brings to mind another meaning for intuitiveness and that is knowing. I seem to have a keen sense of knowing when it concerns one's health.

When I am healing someone, I am given intuitive information as well as visual holograms. I feel that this is because of the inter-connectedness of everyone. A television would be a good analogy for this. From the same remote control device, you can change the channels and connect to totally different movies.

When I go into a person, I don't have to manually change the channels; they are changed instantaneously by thought. I believe that the information I access is coming from the field of quantum information.

To further the analogy of the television, suppose that all you want to watch is a particular movie. Now imagine that you have a control device that can read your thoughts. The control would pick up your thought and instantaneously go to the movie. This is very similar to when I scan a person for injuries or diseases.

The controls that I use are extremely advanced and sophisticated. I might tune into the person's doctor's information, the person's mother, or someone who has nothing to do with the person, but knows about the injury. All the information obtained is pertinent to the injury and becomes part of my analysis. In this way I am connecting to the field of quantum information for my healing.

Much of the time I use my own non-medical terms to describe what I can see in a person. I looked at a lady who had a total hysterectomy. She had endometriosis (growth of uterine lining outside the uterus) and had growths on other organs from it. She had the hysterectomy 10 years ago and some of the tissue was still located outside of the uterus. The doctors said they could do nothing about it. The tissue I saw had connected to the kidneys as an external growth. The only way I could describe what I saw was that it looked like a plant growing on the outside of the kidneys, which at the time seemed strange to me. But after she described her history, it all made sense.

Another lady had a problem with fluid in her lungs. She said that she could feel the fluid but was unable to cough it up. I went in and looked at her lungs. I described that inside of her lungs looked like they were sealed with some kind of coating. The liquid that she felt in her lungs was behind this coating. She then informed me that she had an operation for breast cancer and the doctors had to apply a sealant on the inside of her lungs after the operation. This would explain what I originally saw in her lungs.

The image information that I receive is not always exactly as it appears physically, which can be a challenge for me. A person that I looked at had damaged disks in his lower back. What I saw was his lower spine being held in place by two thin perpendicular strings. My interpretation of this was instability in the lower back. He confirmed that his doctor had told him exactly that only a few days prior to me seeing him.

The information I receive is not in words, but images. They must be interpreted into something I can explain. This intuitive ability to receive images goes hand-in-hand with the healing. I visually see what and where the problem is, and I collect the intuitive information to complete my healing treatment.

Intuitive abilities are becoming a major part of my energetic healing and diagnosis. At this point, when someone just mentions a name of someone, I am able to pick up information which lets me know what the problems are and whether I am able to help.

Sometimes I receive information which doesn't directly have to do with the injury. I gave a lady one treatment and then didn't hear from her. I knew it had helped her, but I also knew that her husband was against it and was trying to talk her out of it. She eventually did contact me again, and when I mentioned it to her, she wanted to know *how* I knew that. Her husband had indeed tried to talk her out of it, but she had decided to proceed because her arthritis had improved so much after just one treatment. Since then it has improved considerably.

When I look at a person I can tell whether they will be receptive to energy healing or not. I can also tell if it is a person's time. There isn't much that I can do if this is the case. When the body decides that it can't hang on any more, it shows signs of shutting down. This is very evident to me and I feel that it would be futile to try and reverse it. I can give them energy and in some cases help them become more accepting of the inevitable.

I feel that I am constantly in touch with the field of quantum information. It doesn't take much thinking for me to quickly connect to a certain area of the hologram. I also believe that this will get stronger as I get older and more experienced.

Insights

Being able to tap into the field of quantum information opens my consciousness up to receive information about many things. The information available is vast.

Sometimes I receive knowledge about events to occur in the near or distant future. I feel the mind does some sort of an instantaneous statistical analysis of all the sources of information available and narrows it all down to a probable event to take place. This is similar to the ability that Edgar Cayce had to make some amazing predictions.

Edgar Cayce (1877-1945) was one of the most amazing psychics ever. He was able to diagnose illness in people he had never met, and then would prescribe the medical treatment to heal them. He was also a devout Christian who wrote volumes of studies on how clairvoyance and reincarnation are not in contradiction to the teachings of the Bible. I recommend the reading of his material to anyone with an interest in this. Edgar Cayce also became renowned for his ability to make predictions about both physical and spiritual events. Many, but not all of his predictions happened.

The different results probably happened because what he predicts is in a snapshot of time. If everything was to happen exactly as foreseen from this moment in time, then the prediction would come true.

Use a horse race for an analogy. A person reads the statistics on a horse and there is no way it can lose the race. All the other horses are real duds and the horse you want to bet on won the Kentucky Derby once. The track is dry and this is when your horse does its best. For an instant in time, everything points to your horse easily winning the race. As the race gets underway your favorite horse gets bumped by another horse causing it to break an ankle. Well, so much for that prediction. Unforeseen events altered what seemed like a predictable outcome.

The same thing applies to psychic predictions except with more information being utilized. The closer the prediction date is to the present, the more statistically likely it is to happen. I was driving home one night with my Dad around ten o'clock. All of a sudden I told my Dad that "I feel death coming." I said it was a horrible feeling and that hundreds of people were going to die soon. He told me not to worry about it and that we could check the newspapers in the morning. However my Dads' driving became more cautious as he was beginning to wonder if we were about to be involved in an accident.

The next morning when we read the newspaper, we learned that an airplane had left Taipei at 3:00 p.m. and went off the radar screen about 20 minutes after takeoff. Over 200 people died in the crash. We checked the time zone difference and it was exactly when I had the feeling of death coming. There could have been a person onboard the plane who allowed the energy connection to me. It could also have been a result of so many people heading for death at once, and knowing it.

REINCARNATION

"We have all died many times and will continue to live and die. Our path is defined by our accumulated intentions."

- Adam

At first, reincarnation was very difficult for me to accept and I probably risk losing some readers when discussing it. It is hard enough to accept that I can heal people without touching them. I am not a Buddhist and I haven't read much on Buddhism. My views on reincarnation come solely from my insights and ability to see the past lives of others and myself.

We have all had many different lives in the past. Sometimes our illnesses can have something to do with one of our past lives. I also feel that some of the scars we obtain throughout our life have some relationship with something that happened to us when we were in another life.

Many people have experienced deja vu. Visiting another country and feeling a deep connection to a place you have never visited before happens to many people. Sometimes it happens when you meet someone for the first time. You can have a sense of familiarity, as if you have known the person for a long, long time. Sometimes it can create uneasiness when you meet someone, almost like a fear of being around them that you cannot explain. Or how about the times you find yourself coming up with information you never realized you knew? There are numerous indications that this is not the first time we have been here.

I am actually able to see the past lives that people have experienced. When I go in to someone, I usually see present injuries as well as old injuries. I have yet to find someone who doesn't have something wrong. However, every person has a bright white light inside him or her which I can go into. When I go into this white light it looks like a pure body without any scars or injuries. Maybe this represents what we refer to as the soul.

From this bright light I am able to access a person's past lives. There are so many past lives, I seem to access a different one every time I go in. When I see these past lives, I receive some very vivid details. I looked at my Dad and saw him at war with troops that carried a British flag with a battalion number. I have also seen him as a fisherman who lost his life at sea. My Dad has always been terrified of swimming in deep water, and I don't think that this fear is coincidental.

Sometimes our past lives are not what we might want them to be. I went into the past life of a friend and saw that he was a sheep farmer overlooking the ocean. There is nothing wrong with being a sheep farmer, but people expect something more glamorous. They wish they had been a king or queen in a past life. Whatever your past consists of, it makes up the person you are now. You are like a quilt fabricated from many different patterns to make something that is beautiful.

Open Mindedness

A person can be both open-minded and skeptical at the same time. One has to be careful that they don't become so committed to skepticism that all ability to be open-minded is lost. Good researchers require an open and inquiring mind. There is no shortage of formal published scientific studies to support the validity of distant healing. The mere mention of distant healing to most people is almost considered taboo. Even professed open-minded people have no interest in learning about this amazing ability.

It is especially difficult for me to face this rejection from people, since I actually experience my special gift every day. It has fuelled my ambition to educate and inform the world about the existence of these abilities. Almost every scientific inventor was ridiculed by their contemporaries. It was only later in their lives that they became great men in the eyes of the world.

> *"Censorship and character assassination*
> *are ways to discredit anyone who suggests*
> *that reality exists beyond our five senses."*
> *Frank 2002*

Take Alexander Graham Bell for instance. He invented the phone and had a very difficult time finding anyone interested in it. The chief engineer Sir William Preece at British Post said, "England has plenty of small boys to run messages." Sir William Preece was a Fellow of the Royal Society who had studied under the great Michael Faraday.

Sir Preece outdid this judgement when Thomas Edison announced that he invented an electric light. Preece described it as "A completely idiotic idea."

The best example of all has to be the Wright brothers. They actually had photographs of them flying their plane, many public demonstrations along with local dignitaries watching. It was still dismissed as a hoax by most American scientists and top science magazines.

Here are a few other skeptical quotes:

"There is no need for any individual to have a computer in their home."
**- Ken Olson, 1977, President
Digital Equipment Corp.**

"I think there is a world market for maybe five computers."
**- Thomas Watson
Chairman of IBM, 1943.**

"Radio has no future."
- Lord Kelvin, ca. 1897.

"Well informed people know it is impossible to transmit the voice over wires and that were it possible to do so, the thing would be of no practical value."
- Editorial in the Boston Post (1865)

"Heavier-than-air flying machines are impossible."
- Lord Kelvin, ca. 1895
British mathematician and physicist

An American politician in the 1800's made this statement (in the name of cost cutting):

"We might as well shut down the patent offices because everything that can be invented has been invented."

Thankfully, our searching has led to a number of well-educated people who are very knowledgeable and willing to help us understand this ability that could benefit the whole world. They are courageous people. It takes a very strong individual to go against the mainstream thinking and pursue answers to the many unexplained events around us. I truly respect these people and hope they will be vindicated someday from all the attacks by their critics.

It is interesting how people that I have known all my life are so doubtful when I explain distant healing. The most reassuring thing about all the skepticism I have experienced is that most people can eventually understand and accept this concept. I have changed the thinking of many people simply by demonstrating what I do. When a person actually feels sensation in their body from a distant healing and notices a definite change in their health, they find it difficult to deny that it works. Of course there are people who are skeptics just for the sake of being skeptical. I almost feel an obligation to change their thinking, because it seems like such a shame for someone to go through life and miss out on something so simple yet so profound. There is joy in the healing of a person and there is also joy from changing person's views on distant healing. I am unable to heal everyone but I can make people aware of the existence of this connection, which we all potentially have access to. The "7 Steps for Life" section in the next chapter will help you to unlock your own self-healing ability.

PEOPLE HAVE MUCH MORE
Power AND CONTROL THAN THEY
SEEM TO REALIZE.

Adam

CHAPTER 9

Living Well

Everything IS INTERCONNECTED
AND ONE CHANGE OR
DYSFUNCTION AFFECTS
EVERYTHING ELSE.

Adam

Living Well

Despite my youth and apparent lack of experience, at least in this life, I know these things intuitively. It is essential that we all find happiness in our every day lives. A positive approach to life and all that it brings will ensure that good things happen. And this in turn equates to better health. Research has proven that positive feelings not only reduce the levels of stress hormones, but wounds heal significantly faster. That is because positive feelings make the immune system stronger and give it direction. Negative feelings and emotions have been proven to weaken the immune system.

Difficulties or challenges are daily occurrences. Severe problems occur from time to time. What makes the difference for us is not so much what the details of the problem are, but how it is handled and perceived by YOU.

How you react to something is more important than *what* is happening. And that's where people have much more power and control than they seem to realize. You always have a choice as to how you are going to react. And your choice can often, if not always, strongly influence the outcome.

You can always, always, always choose your attitude. Your attitude determines how you react to something. It also determines how much stress is attached to a situation. People bring on much more stress into their lives than they need to, simply by inappropriate reactions to situations. By choosing different attitudes (reactions) stress levels can immediately diminish. If you really think about it, few situations in life merit an 'over the top' reaction. It is good to learn to relax, go with the flow, and enjoy the simple pleasures of life.

It is also very helpful if you can approach life with a sense of humor. Kids are naturals at this. The average kid laughs or chuckles about 146 times a day. The average adult only does this about four times a day. Big difference!

Children also know how to enjoy the simpler pleasures, such as splashing in puddles simply because they are there. The reason is that they have a different concept of time and its passing. It wouldn't occur to young children to concern themselves with the fact that they might get wet or dirty from puddle splashing. They live in the moment of the fun in action, appreciating the present tense of time, or NOW. Future concerns, consequences and worries don't even enter into their psyche. Children live in the present. Somehow over time we lose this perspective, which is essential to maintaining health.

I believe it is lost when our lives become controlled by time.

We start school at a certain age during a certain time of the year, on a predetermined day at a prescheduled time. TIME is all of a sudden of extreme importance to us even though our understanding of it is still very vague.

In school some days, time passes quickly, like on sports days. On other days time slows down, such as it does when we are supposed to learn something in which we are not the least bit interested. Time varies a great deal on the same day, depending on our interest level in the current activity. The academic part of school passes slowly, but then at lunchtime, it passes so quickly that sometimes we hardly have time to eat let alone get a good game going before the bell rings.

The afternoon in school has to be the slowest that time could possibly move without standing still. By this time, all the hyperactive kids have had enough of sitting. *Finally* the bell rings, and happy yelps of *freedom* echo through the hallways. The next couple of hours skip by in seconds before we have to be home for dinner.

Gradually we learn how to tell time and most kids eventually get a watch as an essential item to have with them at all times. Time is no longer told to us by the sound of the school bell ringing, or when the streetlights turn on. It is now a very precise measurement of something called time. No longer does Mom gently wake us from dream state. We have now grown up enough to have our personal alarm clock scream in our own ears at a designated time. Each day starts with an incredible (and unnatural) adrenaline shock to our system.

As we become adults, we are conditioned to equate time with money. TIME IS MONEY, we are told. We are expected to get jobs that have specific hours of work. The normal workday starts at 9:00 a.m., lunch is noon to 1:00 p.m., and the day ends at 5:00 p.m. So the workday schedules our time and events for five days out of every week.

7:00 a.m.	ALARM, wake up, shower, etc.
7:30 a.m.	Breakfast.
8:00 a.m.	Catch the bus to work or drive.
8:45 a.m.	Get to work early, looking sharp!
9:00 a.m.	Workday begins
12 Noon	Hungry or not, it's LUNCHTIME
1:00 p.m.	Back to work.
5:00 p.m.	Day Ends. Commuting begins.
5:30 p.m.	Get home. Start making dinner.
6:00 p.m.	EAT, whether hungry or not.
6:30 p.m.	Chores & evening activities.
10:00 p.m.	Wind down so we can wake up at 7:00 a.m. AND START THE WHOLE THING AGAIN.

In short, we wake at a specific time, not when our bodies tell us that we feel adequately rested. Many people keep functioning without enough sleep but relentlessly keep in stride with clock time. This chronic situation is a major contributor of stress in our society. Fatigue is epidemic and it leads to errors in judgment, accidents, strained relationships, frayed nerves, and deteriorating health.

We eat when we have a designated time slot available for it, not necessarily when we are hungry. If you ask some people if they are hungry, they will look at their watch before they answer. Eating becomes an activity within our off time. This may lead to overeating as a habit, hobby or social pastime. It is seen as beyond something that our bodies require.

This may result in addictive behavior, which can lead to obesity, a growing health problem in our society. Eating can easily become a comfort zone activity during scheduled time out. It becomes an activity we treasure because it is beyond the bounds of our stressful time-constraint day.

Many notions of time measurement create stress for us. In school, exams must be written at specific times, which may not be the time of day in which we function most effectively. But we do it to avoid failing, because we must keep up with our grades.

People who have been told by their doctors that they are terminally ill are given a life sentence. If someone is told that they have 6 - 12 months to live, many will die within this prescribed time as if it is an indisputable fact. We tend to forget that nobody knows this as fact and of all people on the face of the Earth, YOU have the most to say and do about this YOURSELF.

It is a well know fact in medicine that patients will often hang on to life until they are able to see someone important or significant to them. Earlier in this book I talked about a gentleman who recovered sufficiently from a stroke until all his significant family members were able to assemble for dinner at his favorite restaurant. This often happens. We have more control than we are sometimes led to believe.

The point is, if we don't want to hear something, we can always choose not to listen. If something is doing us psychological harm, such as being told that we are going to die in six months, then we can deflect it. Always take the opportunity to EMPOWER yourself. The truth is, you have the power until or unless you choose to give it to someone else.

We can learn a great deal from little children with regards to the importance of time. Almost every preschooler could give us the following valuable advice, through their actions: LET TIME BE. This is particularly hard for Type A personalities, or high-strung individuals but the best thing they could do is leave their watches at home. Our societal obsession with creating structured time is the ultimate source of many illnesses. Time is only structured through the eye of the beholder: YOU!

Seven Steps for Life

1. Feel your own energy and be aware of it.

In order to feel your own energy, rub your palms together in a circle. Be sure to get the spot right in the center of your palms. Feel the generation of heat. It is your own energy. Then place your palms an inch apart and feel the magnetic push and pull feelings. Move your palms further apart until you can no longer feel your energy field. Play with your energy and have fun with it. Our energy system is what this is all about, so become aware of it.

This flow of energy is our life force. It is more important than any other body system, as it involves all of them. Better known are our digestive, respiratory, circulatory, metabolic and nervous systems. We have created lots of tests to measure the efficiency and health level of each of these. Since we have yet to develop a measurable level for our energy system, it is ignored. Yet, it directly affects *all* aspects of our health. Learn to feel it, work with it, and most of all - enjoy it.

2. Breathe abdominally and be aware of it.

Breathe deeply. Many people usually breathe very shallow breaths and are actually somewhat oxygen deprived.

The body gets enough to function, but not as much as it would with full, deep breaths. Singers and athletes are very aware of how proper breathing enhances their performance. Air is necessary for all of us to reach our own maximum potential.

Breathe in through your nose and imagine filling your abdomen with air. Once full, exhale through your mouth and pull in your belly. Your shoulders should not go up and down with breathing. It may take a bit of time for you to develop good breathing habits, but stay with it. I know some people that make a point of deep breathing as they go for their daily walk. They count to four as they inhale, hold for another four and breathe out over four counts, increasing the count as their lung capacity expands over time. This is a good exercise to practice proper breathing.

3. *Ground your energy and be aware of its flow.*

It is important to ground your energy often. Think of your energy as circulating through and around you, connecting you to the universal energy above and below the earth. With each breath, breathe in air and energy from above and around you. When exhaling, imagine forcing that energy down the front of your body, through the soles of your feet to the center of the Earth. Feel your soles connecting to the Earth's core. The exhale connects you to everything on the planet. The inhale connects you with all in the universe. This is grounding, which is all about being aware of our connection to energy systems. Grounding will increase your physical energy and strength by unifying your aura with other energy systems. It will cleanse your aura and generally improve your health.

4. Drink water.

Drink water. Lots of it! We are water-based creatures. Everyday drink the 8 glasses your body needs. We are nearly 80 percent water and we must respect this. Coffee, tea, milk and pop are NOT substitutes for water. Drink filtered water only, if possible. If you want to taste something more exciting, add a twist of fresh lime or lemon.

You would never think of trying to run your car without adding oil and gas. Why would you treat a machine with more respect and care than you would your own body? We have been given this fabulously effective body, and it shouldn't be taken for granted.

5. Develop emotional bonds with others.

Many of us, but not all, are fortunate enough to have loving family members. Yet at any moment in time, each and every one of us has the opportunity to bond with others as friends. We all need these emotional connections. It requires a give-and-take of trust to make relationships work, but it is well worth the effort. Welcome it and your world becomes a wonderful, loving place to live filled with good, harmonious energy.

Stable and loving relationships have been shown to have a strong and positive influence on health. Those who have made the effort and commitment to develop close relationships with family members and/or friends are healthier. If they do get sick or experience an injury, they recover much faster than people who do not have a network of supportive family and/or friends.

6. *Think positively in the present tense and feel its effects.*

The power of your own positive thoughts helps to balance your mental, physical, emotional and spiritual aspects. This balance empowers each of us, making us able to achieve our dreams and keep us healthy. Stay in the now as the past is over and fears about the future are futile.

Dream of what you truly love to do and DO IT. Only you can make a lasting change in yourself. By looking inward, it is possible to re-create yourself. Be aware of your feelings and your power to adjust and control them.

Put yourself into a quiet meditative state. Picture a three dimensional holographic image of yourself. This takes lots of concentration and practice, but once you master it, you will notice the benefit. Make it a perfect image of yourself. If your eyes are blue, imagine the image of yourself with blue eyes. Visualize it. Concentrate on seeing your eyes exactly as they look. Work on perfecting this image until it is a PERFECT image of you. Make it perfect in every little detail. Even someone who lacks imagination can do this.

Once you have this clear image in the front of your mind, repeat to yourself that you are all better and problem-free. Have this beam of positive thoughts concentrate on the injured area. For example, if you have an elbow problem, project these positive thoughts like a laser beam towards your elbow.

DO NOT think of the problems. You do not have any problems in the image you have put in front of you. Think of the already perfect hologram with no injuries getting even more perfect. I know this can work for you because of what I do. I heal people with my ability to connect to their energy hologram. Once I connect to a person, I use my thoughts to perform the healing work that I do.

I understand that this ability to connect to a person's hologram is a gift. I also know that we all have the ability to make the connection to our own hologram and use the power of thought to heal. This does not come easy, but with the desire to learn and with some practice you will succeed. By continuing to practice, you will find that it gets easier and easier, and that your ability to do this increases. Most people will find this a very effective method to maintain their state of wellness.

7. *Understand (and appreciate) the connectedness of everything and everyone.*

Like a web, everything affects everything else in the entire universe. Positive thoughts and actions taken by one of us affects everyone else, with the most affected being the closest to us in the web (family, friends, work mates, acquaintances) but the entire web is affected. It is this interconnectedness that enables distant healing to take place.

Feel grateful for your life — it is precious. Be thankful for all of the wonderful people that have connected with you along your journey. Look forward to the adventures that each day brings. We all face challenges and be grateful for them as well. The positive outlook of each of us is contagious.

NOETIC BET
REALITY IS MORE THAN MERELY PHYSICAL.
EVERYTHING AND EVERYONE ARE
INTERCONNECTED.
WE CAN CONSCIOUSLY PARTICIPATE IN
OUR OWN EVOLUTION.
IONS Newsletter 2003

Chapter 10

Your Dream

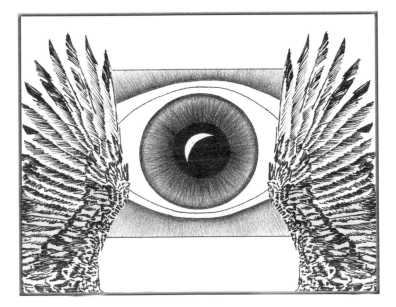

THERE ARE MANY THINGS THAT WE DON'T UNDERSTAND AND SCIENCE CANNOT YET EXPLAIN THEM.

Adam

YOUR DREAM

"Dreams are part of our heart and soul
Our dreams go to the depths of our thoughts,
Wants, and needs to fulfill our destiny,
In order to fulfill our destiny we must
Fulfill our dreams."
— J.R. Davis, 1994

I have helped many people and the most enjoyable part is receiving their appreciation. It is such a pleasure to have them understand the connection that we have shared. I have received many testimonials from people who understand and accept that their health has improved. This showing of gratitude inspires me to help others. When I help a grandfather with cancer I know I am not only helping him, but also his wife, daughters, sons, grandchildren and good friends. The wellness affects as many people as the sickness did.

I am living my dream.

I am always amazed and somewhat amused at the response I get from people when I tell them of my abilities. If someone asks me to explain my ability I might say, "I do distant healing by connecting to the quantum hologram of another person."

Friends I have known all my life and relatives react in a similarly unusual manner. Often the subject is totally dismissed or deflected with their response being along the lines of "lovely weather we are having, isn't it?"

Those who are receptive and understand what I do often find themselves in the same predicament of trying to explain it to others. It's almost as if it is taboo to talk about something that doesn't fit into the mainstream of thinking. We all have to change this mentality in order for humankind to advance at a conscious level — the level of knowing and understanding everything within us and around us.

People must usually be alone with me for it to be possible to engage in a conversation about the topic. When there is more than one person, there seems to be a giggle factor which kicks in. It is a form of human self-defense if our brains can't stretch far enough to grasp an idea or concept.

Accepting change or a new way of thinking is referred to as a paradigm shift. There have been many examples of dramatic paradigm shifts throughout civilization and there is no reason to believe that there won't be many more.

I always thought that one characteristic of humankind that prevents us from moving forward is our ego. A dramatic example of how our ego can have a major impact on how we perceive things is the Ptolemaic system. Scientists proclaimed that the universe rotated around the Earth. With billions and billions of stars and planets in the sky, how much bigger can one's ego be! But nonetheless, this scientific proclamation was widely accepted.

The Ptolemaic system was so accepted that many people were put to death for thinking differently. We might find that shocking, but what it really should do is remind us that we must continue to question today's science and not just accept it. We must always be able to subjectively analyze knowledge beyond our current scientific base of information. We should learn from our past and not blindly accept all current science as truth. We've been mistaken before.

One example of a paradigm, which I find amusing, has to do with elephants. If you tether an elephant to a small post with a rope that is simply placed over the top of it, *the elephant is unable to move away.*

Despite the fact that it is not tied, and even though the elephant with its massive weight could easily pull the post from the ground, the elephant will not move. In its mind, it thinks that it is securely tethered and can't possibly pull away. Obviously that couldn't be further from the truth, because all the elephant has to do is walk away. This analogy can easily be applied to our day-to-day thinking about what is possible and impossible. Our limitations are self-imposed.

There is a swell of change taking place in the world today. With freedom comes the ability to question the medical and scientific dogma that we confront on a daily basis. It wasn't long ago that you wouldn't dare tell your doctor that you would like a second opinion. Today, many doctors go out of their way to explain your medical diagnosis in detail in order to meet the demands of the inquiring patient. This is, in a small way, a paradigm shift. People are finally coming to the realization that doctors really aren't gods, yet their opinions should be respected. The ultimate health choices are one's own responsibility.

More and more of us are becoming aware of people with special abilities. There are many things that we don't understand and science cannot yet explain them. We are coming to the realization that if science can't explain it, this doesn't mean it's impossible.

The toughest belief to change is that we think experts are all open-minded and willing to explore new science. Even top scientists have built paradigms around themselves that are impossible for them to breach. Change is difficult and humans resist change.

However, we must change in order to move forward and this will happen naturally when the critical mass of consciousness is reached. This means that when enough people become aware of our connectedness, our conscious awareness will change with it.

One force joins us. One idea keeps us apart. Love is the unifying force. Fear is the underlying separation of beings. The future of mankind depends on how we apply this unifying force. Love and cooperation is needed.

Fear and material competition must be left in the past with ego. This only intensifies our perception of separateness, which leads to conflict. Human survival is the ultimate goal of every being and can be accomplished when our commonality is our focus, not our differences.

My personal goal is to make people realize that many things exist beyond our five senses. We have to be able to open our mind's eye and see beyond the societal and scientific paradigms that exist in our world. Everyone must become fully aware of our interconnectedness and only then will we be able to heal ourselves. Believe in yourself and everything becomes possible. There is more to this universe than we know.

STAY TUNED!!

AfterWords

by
Rachel Orr

The other day I noticed an elderly woman walking with her dog. He was old, too, and they seemed to make a good pair. However, as I got nearer to them, I could tell that she was frustrated with his interest in every blade of grass as he slowly meandered across the parkway. I know she was probably anxious to get home, but I also could tell that the dog was really enjoying his foray. As I reached earshot, I smiled.

"What a great dog!" I said to her. "And how lucky he is to have you to take him for a walk. He is sure enjoying himself."

She looked at me and stopped in her tracks. Then she smiled.

"Yes, he is a great companion for me since my husband passed away last year," she replied.

As they walked away, I saw that she had slowed her pace and was talking kindly to her 'companion.' And I swear the dog looked at me and I saw gratitude in his eyes. It was as if he *knew* what I had done, and appreciated it.

I believe all living beings — human, plant or animal — are connected and all benefit if one benefits. In a small way, life got better for all three of us involved in this brief interaction. The old gal felt better about her walk and remembered how much she appreciated her canine friend. He had a much more enjoyable, and probably longer walk. And I felt better watching the impatience leave her face and seeing the gratitude in his. I often think about how much the world would improve if we all made something a little bit better in some way every day.

I believe that everything happens for a reason. It is no more of a coincidence that you are reading this book than it was that Adam found me and I had the wonderful, unforgettable experience of working with him on this book. In many ways, it has changed me forever. My understanding of our interconnectedness has deepened, and my thoughts turn to one of my favorite fantasies; a world in which everyone is keenly aware of the interconnectedness of all living forms.

It would change the world.

It would make many other things possible, too, like peaceful co-existence of all peoples. We would see that we are all in this together, regardless of race, creed, religion, tribal affiliation or any other concept that is based on separation, because separation inevitably gives rise to that insidious attitude of "us" against "them." There is only "we."

In this fantasy world, the planet and its rich resources would be respected and managed with responsible stewardship. If we all felt the interconnectedness, we would do no less. Yes, in my ideal, albeit yet fantasy world, that one simple principle — *we all are connected to all there is* — would cause many wonderful changes.

We would be kind to each other, and within the ensuing harmony who knows what else we could achieve and become. I know one thing for sure, it all starts between our ears. What we think has so much to do with what is created in our reality.

So does our attitude. Having a positive expectation of an outcome highly increases the probability of the event. So does a negative expectation. And given that we have a choice (no one ever can force us to have either), choosing a positive attitude is simply logical, in my opinion.

I hope that you have learned and been inspired, because that was Adam's intent in putting this book together. Remember there is always hope, no matter how difficult your situation seems. Believe and hold on to that belief. And never forget that there is always something you can do. You have the power.

I hear a lot of talk about self-empowerment lately. I support the concept of a powerful self, but I think we should realize that we already have the power. We only lose it if we give it to someone else.

Adam is truly a remarkable young man. Healing ability is one of his gifts. I have experienced it first hand. You might expect that someone with his abilities and powers would be arrogant or distant. He isn't. In fact he is far from either. He is humble, charming, warm and wise beyond his years. He is grounded, stable and full of life as any 16-year-old should be. And he has a great sense of humor.

His parents are also unforgettable. I will always remember my once a week get-togethers with his Mom, who has become my friend. We shared so much during our times together, and I always left with a wonderful feeling of wellness. You can't be around this family and not feel great. They are all special people.

Projects like this don't come together without dedication and cooperation from many sources. Our thanks to the craftsmen who applied their talents in the physical production of it, from typesetting to printing. Thanks to mates and friends for their patience and understanding while we were preoccupied with this manuscript.

And above all, thanks to Adam for being who he is, and for so openly sharing himself. If this is what he is capable of at 16 years, it is exciting to imagine his potential. One of his greatest gifts is that of a visionary. I have always loved the quote "Vision is the ability to see what isn't there." If that's true, I have a feeling Adam will be showing us what we have not yet seen. I look forward to the journey!

— Rachel Orr

To purchase additional copies of DreamHealer, visit
www.dreamhealer.com

Distributed by:
Hampton Roads Publishing Company
who publishes and distributes books on a variety of subjects,
including metaphysics, health, integrative medicine,
visionary fiction, and other related topics.

To order or receive a copy of their latest catalog, call toll-free,
800-766-8009, or send your name and address to:

Hampton Roads Publishing Company, Inc.
1125 Stoney Ridge Road
Charlottesville, VA 22902